Labor Force Participation: Recent Developments and Future Prospects

I. Introduction

More than five years after the Great Recession ended, the labor market has, by many metrics, finally shown substantial improvement. The unemployment rate is now nearly 4 percentage points below the peak reached in late 2009, and the number of nonfarm payroll jobs has returned to pre-recession levels. However, one lingering concern is the ongoing decline in the labor force participation rate and the concomitant absence of a significant rise in the percentage of the working-age population who are employed. In particular, the labor force participation rate has fallen from about 66 percent of the population in 2007 to about 63 percent over the first half of 2014, while the employment-to-population ratio currently stands at 59 percent, only about ½ percentage point above its low point in the wake of the recession (figure 1).

To an important extent, this decline in the labor force participation rate likely reflects the ongoing influence of the aging population that was the focus of a Brookings Paper written nearly a decade ago, whose authors included a subset of us (Aaronson et al., 2006). Indeed, in that paper, we predicted further declines in the participation rate over the subsequent decade as the population continued to age and the baby-boom generation continued to enter their retirement years. However, population aging cannot account for the entire decline in the aggregate participation rate, and the deep recession that was precipitated by the financial crisis, along with the slow economic recovery that has followed, have led some observers to ask whether cyclical factors may have played an important role as well – and, if so, whether many individuals who dropped out of the labor force because they became discouraged about their job prospects may eventually re-enter the workforce as the labor market continues to strengthen.

The answers to these questions have important implications for government policies. If much of the decline in the participation rate can be reversed (or a further decline prevented) by a sufficiently tight labor market, then policymakers should arguably take the low level of the participation rate into account in designing countercyclical policy actions. However, some of the decline in the participation rate may not be amenable to countercyclical policies. We will refer to this portion of the decline as "structural" in nature, and these structural factors present a different set of challenges for policymakers. To the extent that they are caused by obstacles faced by individuals who would like to work or disincentives to work, policymakers would be well-advised to look for other ways to mitigate them. However, some of these structural factors may be unpreventable (such as aging of the population) or undesirable to reverse (such as higher school enrollment rates among the young), leading to a slower growth rate of potential output. Yet, despite the significant policy implications, the range of views on these questions is surprisingly wide.

In this paper, we provide an in-depth analysis of the sources of the decline in the participation rate over the past decade or so. Our primary aim is to assess explanations for this recent decline in participation. However, since participation rates have been falling for some demographic groups since well before the recession began, at times our analysis necessarily extends to earlier periods in order to properly frame more recent developments.

We take two separate approaches to assessing the recent decline. First, we examine a number of specific explanations for the decline in participation using a variety of analyses. We begin by assessing the importance the of aging of the population, which *a priori* seems likely to have been a significant contributor to the decline in the aggregate participation rate. We then examine measures of degree of labor market attachment and use cross-state panel regressions to assess how much of the decline in participation may be the product of the recession and subsequent slow recovery that could be reversed as the economy strengthens further. We then turn to assessing the importance of several other developments that have been noted elsewhere, such as the decline in participation for teenagers and young adults and less-educated prime-age adults, and changes in retirement and disability rates, with an eye towards understanding how these developments have affected the decline in aggregate participation over the short and medium run, and whether they might be reversed going forward.

In order to account for these (and other) factors in a unified framework, our second approach to assessing the decline in labor force participation builds off of a model of the participation rate that had its genesis in the earlier Brookings paper mentioned above. This model attempts to simultaneously capture the contributions of aging, the business cycle, other measurable factors – such as changes in life expectancy, educational attainment, Social Security generosity, and marriage and fertility rates – and birth-cohort-specific factors that we have not so far identified.

Combining the results from these different approaches, our overall assessment is that much – but not all – of the decline in the labor force participation rate since 2007 is structural in nature. As a result, while policymakers can view some of the current low level of the participation rate as indicative of labor market slack beyond that indicated by the unemployment rate alone, they should not expect the participation rate to show a substantial increase from current levels as labor market conditions continue to improve. Indeed, as we show in the final section of the paper, projections from our model point to further declines in the trend participation rate over the next decade or so.

II. Alternative views of the recent decline in labor force participation

The prominence of the decline in the labor force participation rate since 2007, along with its importance for policymakers, has fueled a substantial flow of recent research, as well as more general commentary, on this topic. While an extensive review of this literature is beyond the scope of this paper, as a prelude to our own analysis we first provide a relatively brief summary of some of the recent research that has attempted to shed light on the causes of the recent decline in participation, highlighting the wide range of often contradictory conclusions reached in these studies.[1]

In our view, observers should not have been particularly surprised by the fact that the labor force participation rate has declined noticeably over the past seven years. As noted above, our earlier Brookings paper, which was written prior to the financial crisis, had highlighted a number of factors that were likely to put downward pressure on labor force participation over the subsequent decade, and indeed, as shown by the dashed line in figure 1, the predictions we made in that paper turned out to track the decline in the actual participation rate quite closely. That said, we readily admit that the severe recession complicates the interpretation of the participation rate decline, and, more generally, we would advise against taking an overly strong signal about the sources of the decline in the aggregate participation rate from our previous forecasts. In particular, although the traditional view on movements in labor force participation over the business cycle generally emphasized the absence of a substantial cyclical response, the breathtaking drop in labor demand in 2008 and 2009 may mean that this time really is different. In that regard, the severity of the Great Recession and the subsequent slow pace of the economic

---

[1] For a more comprehensive survey on recent research on the decline in labor force participation, see Council of Economic Advisers (2014).

recovery have led some researchers to interpret the decline in participation as having a large cyclical component.

A recent paper by Erceg and Levin (2013) provides a prominent example of this line of thought. They first point out that labor force projections made by the BLS in November 2007 went badly off track over the next several years, both for the aggregate participation rate and for several key demographic groups.[2] They supplement that observation with a cross-state regression showing a statistically significant negative correlation between changes in state-level participation rates for prime-age adults from 2007 – 2012 and changes in state-level unemployment rates for this demographic group between 2007 and 2010. Their conclusion from this analysis is that "the aggregate decline in prime-age LFPR can be *fully* explained by the persistent shortfall in labor demand" (p. 15), suggesting that the current level of the unemployment rate significantly understates the extent of labor market slack. While suggestive, a number of caveats pertain to that analysis, as we discuss in section IV, including that their analysis covers a short time period and does not make use of information on the relationship between the unemployment and participation rates in previous episodes.

Another paper in this vein is Hotchkiss and Rios-Avila (2013), who argue "that the dramatic decline in labor force participation during the Great Recession is *more than* explained by deteriorating labor market conditions (cyclical factors)" (p. 1). While acknowledging the downward pressure on participation from the aging of the population, they claim that the

---

[2] Using the BLS projection from November 2007 as a baseline seems somewhat dubious to us, given that their projections of the labor force participation rate trend through 2014 were well above those from our 2006 paper. The BLS projections of labor force participation for specific demographic groups are not projections from a behavioral model, but rather extrapolations of a nonlinear filter used to smooth historical labor force participation rates for each age, gender, race, and ethnicity group (see Toossi, 2011). However, Toossi also reports on her preliminary efforts to construct a behavioral model for projecting the participation rate, which found that the projected values from such a model for the 2007-2009 period were similar to those from the existing BLS model and that both approaches were surprised by the low level of the participation rate in 2009.

participation rate would be even lower had individuals not altered their behavior in structural ways following the recession. In particular, constructing a counterfactual participation rate path using a reweighting approach suggested by DiNardo et al. (1996), they find that, all else equal, greater educational attainment and a reduction in fertility in the wake of the recession caused labor force participation to be higher in recent years than it would have been in the absence of these behavioral responses, masking some of the effects of weak labor demand on the participation rate.

Although Hotchkiss and Rios-Avila attempt to quantify the importance of behavioral responses in participation to some extent, they do not allow for differential participation rates across different cohorts, which we find to be an important factor in the model we present later in the paper. In addition, like Erceg and Levin, these authors base their estimates on a short sample period and thus do not make use of the behavior of the participation rate in other episodes. Finally, they use average weeks worked as an indicator of labor market conditions, which, because of its mechanical relationship with the participation rate, likely biases upward their estimate of the effects of the recession on the change in labor force participation.

At the other end of the spectrum, Kudlyak (2013) uses a barebones version of the cohort-based model we present later in the paper and shows that the actual participation rate in 2012 was quite close to an estimate of the trend participation rate constructed from a model that includes only age-gender fixed effects and birth-year/gender fixed effects, and above a model that takes into account the cyclical deviation of employment from its trend. Although she cautions that the estimated cohort effects may be influenced by both structural and cyclical factors, she interprets her results as suggesting that most of the decline in the participation rate is accounted for by the trend. However, it is difficult to assess that interpretation because she does not include other factors that might cause changes over time in the propensity of different demographic groups to participate in the labor force, as we do below.

Other authors come out somewhere in the middle. For example, Aaronson et al. (2012) estimate a model that allows cohort effects and the coefficients on other controls to differ by age, sex, and educational attainment and find that nearly half of the decline in the participation rate between 2000 and 2011 reflected demographic factors. Similarly, the Council of Economic Advisors recently analyzed potential sources of the decline in participation since 2007 and attributed half of the decline to aging, one sixth to "typical" cyclical weakness, and the remainder to other pre-existing trends or other factors associated with the severity of the recession. A separate analysis by Hall (2014) comes to a similar conclusion, but traces much of the decline beyond that of aging to a combination of an increase in disability recipients and the expansion of the food stamp program, both of which discourage participation by implicitly taxing earnings. Finally, pure time-series methods, such as those employed by Van Zandweghe (2012), Barnes et al. (2013), and Reifschneider et al. (2013), attribute between one half and two-thirds of the decline in participation since 2007 to trend movements, although of course such analyses say little about the underlying sources of a declining trend participation rate.

All of these research papers provide a useful perspective on recent changes in the labor force participation rate. However, as Kudlyak concludes in her paper, "more research is needed that would explicitly model and account for the factors that influence the labor force participation decision of different demographic groups" (pp. 40-41). This is what we attempt to accomplish in this paper. In particular, we think the most promising approach to analyzing participation rate movements would ideally incorporate insights from the voluminous literature on the factors that affect the labor force participation rate. For example, researchers have shown that, in addition to changes in the age distribution of the population and cohort-specific effects, the labor force participation rate is importantly driven by factors specific to labor supply among particular groups, declining market opportunities (for instance labor market polarization) and wage growth, import competition, disability, and retirement decisions. An empirical model that accounts for at least some of these factors is more likely to accurately decompose participation rate movements into cyclical and the structural components than a model that is agnostic about these factors. Moreover, such a model can also enable a more precise identification of driving forces behind structural participation rate trends than embodied in the literature to date.

III. The contribution of changes in the age distribution

Perhaps the determinant of the aggregate participation rate that is easiest to analyze is the changing age distribution of the population. In short, as is well known, the population as a whole has been aging, putting downward pressure on the participation rate as the large baby-boom generation moves into age groups that traditionally have low participation rates.

A "shift-share" calculation of the contribution of aging to the recent declines in the labor force participation rate (LFPR) is straightforward, but, as is often the case, the numbers can differ depending on what one chooses to use as the baseline. The first column of numbers in table 1 shows three such choices.

Note that the first row of that table shows the participation rate data that have been adjusted for periodic changes to population controls and the redesign of the CPS in 1994, in order to provide a more consistent measure of participation, and, to allow for calculations by single-year ages, built up from the CPS microdata and seasonally adjusted. (See section VI for more details.) This differs slightly from the published rate; the latter declined 3.1 percentage points between 2007:Q4 and 2014:Q2, as compared to 2.8 percentage points in our data. We

- 10 -

will refer to the adjusted-basis aggregate rate throughout the paper, although several of the analyses will use unadjusted detailed data.

Table 1: Estimated Contributions from Population Aging to Change in Aggregate LFPR (percentage points)

Type	2007Q4 to 2014Q2	2000Q4 to 2007Q4	1990Q4 to 2000Q4	1976Q4 to 1990Q4
1. Actual LFPR	-2.8	-1.3	+0.2	+4.5
2. Constant LFPR	-1.5	-0.8	-0.3	+0.4
3. Constant Share	-1.3	-0.7	-0.3	+0.8
4. Chain-type	-1.3	-0.7	-0.1	+0.7

Row 2 of the table holds within-age participation rates constant at their 2007:Q4 levels and lets the population share of each age evolve as in the data. Specifically,

(1) Contribution of aging = $\sum_{age,sex} LFPR_{age,sex,2007Q4} * (share_{age,sex,2014Q2} - share_{age,sex,2007Q4})$,

where "age" refers to single years of age from 16 to 79 and those older than 79 are treated as a single group. By this calculation, aging contributed 1.5 percentage points to the total decline of 2.8 percentage points in the aggregate participation rate between the fourth quarter of 2007 and the second quarter of 2014.[3]

Row 3 holds the population share of each age constant and lets the age-specific participation rates evolve as in the data. The portion of the actual change in the participation rate that is not accounted for by this counterfactual is the contribution of aging. That is,

(2) Contribution of aging = $(LFPR_{2014Q2} - LFPR_{2007Q4}) - \sum_{age,sex} share_{age,sex,2007Q4} * (LFPR_{age,sex,2014Q2} - LFPR_{age,sex,2007Q4})$.

$= LFPR_{2014Q2} - \sum_{age,sex} share_{age,sex,2007Q4} * LFPR_{age,sex,2014Q2}$.

---

[3] This and the calculations below actually represent the contribution of changes in the age-sex distribution of the population. However, the contributions of changes in male-female composition of the population are so small that we refer to our calculations simply as the contributions of aging.

By this calculation, aging contributed 1.3 percentage points to the total decline of 2.8 percentage points in the aggregate participation rate.

These two calculations differ, essentially, in their treatment of the cross terms ($\Delta LFPR_{age}$ * $\Delta share_{age}$) and, of course, are sensitive to the particular dates chosen for fixing the weights. Row 4 shows a third option, a chain-type calculation, in which the age-specific participation rates are held constant only month by month.[4] Specifically,

(3) Contribution of aging =

$$\sum_{age,sex} \sum_{m=Oct\ 2007}^{Jun\ 2014} \frac{LFPR_{age,sex,m+1} + LFPR_{age,sex,m}}{2} * \left(share_{age,sex,m+1} - share_{age,sex,m}\right)$$

By this calculation, aging contributed 1.3 percentage points to the total decline of 2.8 percentage points in the aggregate participation rate.

Note that none of these formulas depend directly on changes in within-age participation rates as such over the period in question. However, equations (1) and (2) implicitly assume that the levels of the participation rates in the base year chosen for the calculation are appropriate. As the right-most column of the table illustrates, in some contexts the results can be sensitive to that choice. Equation (3) does not require the choice of a base year. In this sense, that calculation is more robust, and is our preferred formulation. As it happens, however, the three calculations in table 1 do not differ greatly when it comes to the post-2007 period: all indicate that the changing age distribution of the population has been a substantial component of the decline in aggregate labor force participation over this period, with our preferred calculation attributing nearly half of the observed decline to this source.[5]

---

[4] Although we show the result for quarterly participation rates, for technical reasons this index is best calculated from the monthly changes.

[5] Note that the aging of the population has two major components. One is the movement of the large "baby-boom" cohorts from middle to more advanced ages. The other is the ongoing increase in longevity, which would tend to skew the age distribution toward older ages even if all birth cohorts were the same size. However, over this period

The role of the age distribution is of particular interest both because it has been the focus of much of the recent commentary and because its evolution going forward is relatively easy to predict. However, one could perform a similar exercise along several other dimensions, such as educational attainment or marital status, both of which would contribute positively to the change in the participation rate in recent years and thus offset some of the effects of population aging.[6] We attempt to quantify the contributions of these and other factors in section VI.

IV. Assessing the recent cyclicality of labor force participation

As described in the previous section, a simple shift-share analysis suggests that nearly half of the decline in participation since 2007 can be attributed to aging. Another natural explanation for declining participation over the past seven years is the persistently weak labor market. Indeed, it would not be unreasonable to hypothesize that the deep recession and slow pace of recovery led an unusually large number of persons to temporarily drop out of the labor force in recent years because they were discouraged about their job prospects. If so, these persons could return to the labor force when economic conditions improve sufficiently. This section assesses how much the participation rate appears to be cyclically depressed using a number of different approaches.

Reasons for non-participation

We begin with an examination of the reasons labor market nonparticipants report for being out of the labor force. The CPS asks nonparticipants several questions aimed at identifying discouragement, including whether an individual wants a job, is currently available to

---

the latter source accounted for only a small portion of the overall direct contribution of the changing age distribution to the decline in aggregate participation.

[6] See, for example, https://sites.google.com/site/robertshimer/cbo-employment.pdf.

work and has looked for a job in the past 12 months (classified by the BLS as "marginally

attached"), and whether he or she has a job-related reason for not currently looking for work.[7]

While these individuals are not officially counted in the labor force, the data on gross labor

market flows indicate that they have a relatively high probability of moving into the labor force

(we discuss the evidence on gross labor market flows data in section VII).[8]

As indicated in figure 2, three successively stringent measures of labor market

discouragement, defined by the questions noted above, did increase during the Great Recession

and the early stage of recovery, consistent with the explanation of temporary labor market

withdrawal by individuals who faced poor job prospects during cyclical downturns. However,

the share of the population in each of these categories is relatively small, ranging from

0.3 percent for discouraged workers to slightly below 1 percent for the marginally attached and

to 2½ percent for those who say that they want a job. Indeed, judging by the behavior of the

broadest "want job" category, the rise in discouragement could at its peak explain at most

¾ percentage point of the decline in the labor force participation rate since the end of 2007.

The "want job" category appears to have lagged somewhat the unemployment rate during

the Great Recession and peaked at the end of 2012, three years later than the unemployment rate.

This observation suggests that the cyclical component of labor force participation might lag

changes in the unemployment rate, an issue that we investigate more formally below. More

recently, all three measures have declined somewhat, but nevertheless remain elevated,

---

[7] While only persons who satisfy all four criteria are classified by the BLS as "discouraged workers," we will take a more expansive view here.
[8] The discussion here and in the remainder of this section uses data that have not been adjusted for changes to population controls.

suggesting that the labor force participation rate was cyclically depressed in 2014:Q2 by perhaps ½ percentage point due to labor market discouragement as broadly defined.[9]

Evidence from cross-state comparisons of the reasons for nonparticipation suggests a smaller effect of discouragement on the aggregate participation rate. As shown in the top panel of figure 3, the ratio of the state-level shares of nonparticipants who want a job in 2013 relative to the five-year period prior to the financial crisis varies positively with the ratio of state unemployment rates over those periods, consistent with a positive relationship between unemployment and discouragement. However, as shown in the bottom panel, there appears to be no such cross-state relationship between similarly-defined ratios of the labor force participation rate and the unemployment rate. One possible interpretation is that the share of nonparticipants who say that they want a job, and the cyclical variation in that share, is too slight to contribute very much to the overall cyclicality in the aggregate participation rate.[10]

Of course, some amount of discouragement may manifest itself in ways that are unlikely to show up in these measures. For example, business-cycle conditions almost certainly affect individuals' decisions to enroll in school, apply for disability insurance, retire, or to stay home and take care of house or family. And many of these individuals may not report themselves as

---

[9] In addition, using data from 1994 to 2007, based on simple regression of these measures on the unemployment rate gap and its lag, the fraction of marginally attached and discouraged workers are slightly above the levels one would expect given the level of the unemployment rate. We would caution, however, that measurement error may be more acute for these measures of labor market discouragement than with the more familiar measures of unemployment and labor force participation because these more-detailed not-in-labor-force classifications depend on subjective criteria. In particular, prevailing labor market conditions may affect how respondents answer survey questions that are used to determine their status within the nonparticipation category. For example, if wage rates were rising more quickly, more nonparticipants would likely claim that they want a job, indicating that the measures in figure 2 might be understating the true extent of labor market discouragement. In addition, Barnichon and Figura (2013) argue that the share of want-job nonparticipants might have an important secular component, thus making the inference of cyclicality in labor force participation from this category of nonparticipants even more difficult.

[10] Alternatively, this exercise may simply illustrate a broader point, which is that estimates of cyclicality can vary greatly based on the period and technique considered—suggesting that there is inherently a high degree of uncertainty in how much of the recent decline in participation is cyclical and reversible.

wanting a job. However, determining how much of these movements reflect cyclical and how much structural factors is difficult. We will return to some of these issues later in the paper.

Using cross-state variation in the recent changes in unemployment and participation rates

An alternative way to assess the cyclicality in labor force participation in recent years is by exploiting more formally cross-state variation in labor market conditions and the participation rate. In particular, because the severity of the recession varied considerably across states, the correlation between state-level movements in unemployment rates and participation rates may help to identify the effects of the business cycle on participation. Indeed, our 2006 Brookings Paper included such an analysis, and Erceg and Levin (2013) lean heavily on this estimation framework to support their claim that cyclical factors account for a large portion of the decline in participation since 2007.

Table 2: Cross-State Regressions with Unemployment

Dependent variable $\Delta_{2007\text{-}2013}$ LFPR$_i$	(1) 16 to 24 years	(2) 25 to 54 years, men	(3) 25 to 54 years, women	(4) 25 to 54 years, all	(5) 55+ years	(6) all
Panel A						
$\Delta_{2007\text{-}2010}$ Aggr. Unemp. rate	-0.95***	-0.36*	-0.19	-0.29**	-0.44	-0.50***
	(0.22)	(0.20)	(0.14)	(0.14)	(0.33)	(0.16)
Constant	0.08	-0.59	-0.46	-0.48	3.78**	-0.30
	(1.24)	(0.88)	(0.78)	(0.65)	(1.44)	(0.85)
Observations	51	51	51	51	51	51
R-squared	0.23	0.13	0.03	0.12	0.08	0.25
Panel B						
$\Delta_{2007\text{-}2010}$ Aggr. Unemp. rate	-0.27	-0.35	0.29	-0.06	-0.45	-0.28
	(0.34)	(0.28)	(0.20)	(0.20)	(0.42)	(0.22)
$\Delta_{2010\text{-}2013}$ Aggr. Unemp. rate	1.25**	0.01	0.88***	0.43	-0.02	0.41*
	(0.51)	(0.35)	(0.32)	(0.30)	(0.42)	(0.23)
Constant	-0.50	-0.60	-0.87	-0.67	3.79**	-0.49
	(1.18)	(0.94)	(0.69)	(0.64)	(1.47)	(0.88)
Observations	51	51	51	51	51	51
R-squared	0.32	0.13	0.17	0.18	0.08	0.28

Weighted by state population. Standard errors clustered at the state level in parentheses.
*** denotes $p<0.01$, ** $p<0.05$, * $p<0.1$.

We begin by examining cross-state regressions along the lines of those used by Erceg and Levin – that is, by regressing the state-specific change in the participation rate for various demographic groups from 2007 to 2013 on the change in the aggregate unemployment rate from 2007 to 2010, where the latter proxies for the severity of cyclical conditions during the Great Recession.[11] As shown in column (6) in panel A of table 2, the estimated cyclical parameter for the aggregate participation rate is -0.50. For prime-age workers (those 25 to 54 years old, column 4), the estimated cyclical parameter is -0.29, and the cyclicality in participation for prime-age men is greater than for prime-age women. The estimated cyclical effect is especially large for youths, and sizable, but imprecisely estimated for older individuals (55+ years) – groups which Erceg and Levin do not analyze. The constant terms, which can be thought of as

---

[11] In addition to extending their analysis by including data for 2013, our regressions also differ from Erceg and Levin (2013) in the underlying data: we construct state-specific participation and unemployment rates directly from CPS microdata, whereas they use BLS's Local Area Unemployment Statistics (LAUS) data.

an estimate of the trend decline over the 2007-2013 period, are negative but estimated imprecisely; the one exception is for older individuals for whom the estimated trend is positive and statistically significant. Given that the average state unemployment rate rose by 5.0 percentage points between 2007 and 2010, this analysis could be interpreted as suggesting that cyclical factors contributed 2½ percentage points (or 90 percent) to the decline in the aggregate participation rate between 2007 and 2013.

Erceg and Levin (2013) augment their cross-state regressions with a variable measuring the decline in the state unemployment rate from 2010 to 2012. We follow this idea but add in one more year of data and include the decline in the state unemployment rate from 2010 to 2013 in our regressions shown in panel B of table 2. Their results, which are for prime-age adults only (not shown), continue to show a negative and statistically significant effect of the change in the unemployment rate from 2007 to 2010, but essentially no effect of the change in the unemployment rate from 2010 to 2012, which they interpret as evidence that the cyclical decline in participation is highly persistent and thus will respond with a considerable lag to improvements in labor market conditions. In contrast to their findings, in our results for all ages the coefficient on the change in the unemployment rate between 2007 and 2010 remains negative but is much smaller in absolute value (and less precisely measured). In addition, the coefficient on the change in the unemployment rate between 2010 and 2013 is positive and statistically significant. This result could still be consistent with the lagged effects posited by Erceg and Levin (with an even greater lag between the rise in unemployment and the fall in participation than they find), but it also could reflect structural influences that reduced both state unemployment rates and state participation rates over that period. More generally, however, the results from these cross-section regressions do not seem particularly robust to the choice of age group or included years.

Using state-level panel data over a longer period

The regression results in Table 2 are suggestive of important dynamic linkages between unemployment and participation, but further analysis is called for. First, the apparent dynamic relationship points to the need for the explicit inclusion of lagged values of the unemployment rate in the regression specification and the use of panel data. In contrast with the regressions in Table 2, the panel regressions do not assume that the change in unemployment from 2007 to 2010 is the most relevant quantity for all states. This latter point may be important because not all states experienced peak unemployment in 2010, and the pace of unemployment increases and declines differed across states on a year-by-year basis. Second, identifying linkages between participation and unemployment from changes over a single cyclical episode risks confusing them with other idiosyncratic events, such as more generous unemployment insurance benefit durations, or other distortions to labor supply such as the increase in foodstamp take-up noted by Hall (2014). Historical data provide additional variation that can lead to more precise estimates of cyclical elasticity of participation and its dynamics.

In light of these concerns, we next estimate panel state-level regressions using the following specification:

$$LFPR_{s,t} = \alpha_s + \delta_t + \gamma_s time + \lambda LFPR_{s,t-1} + \beta_0 UR_{s,t} + \sum_i \beta_i UR_{s,t-i} + \phi X_{s,t} + \varepsilon_{s,t},$$

where α_s represents state fixed effects, δ_t are time fixed effects, γ_s are state-specific time trends, and X is a vector of covariates related to demographics.[12]

Table 3: Panel Regression Results, CPS Microdata, Annual Frequency

Dependent variable: LFPR	(1) 1978-2013	(2) 1978-2013	(3) 1978-2013	(4) 1978-2013	(5) 1990-2013	(6) 1978-2007
LFPR $_{t-1}$				0.44***	0.35***	0.39***
				(0.03)	(0.03)	(0.03)
Cyclical parameters						
Unemp. rate $_t$	-0.17***	-0.01	-0.07	-0.08**	-0.02	-0.10**
	(0.05)	(0.05)	(0.04)	(0.04)	(0.04)	(0.04)
Unemp. rate $_{t-1}$		-0.10***	-0.06*	-0.07*	-0.06	-0.08**
		(0.03)	(0.03)	(0.04)	(0.05)	(0.04)
Unemp. rate $_{t-2}$		-0.09***	-0.07**	-0.04	-0.03	-0.03
		(0.03)	(0.03)	(0.04)	(0.05)	(0.04)
Unemp. rate $_{t-3}$		-0.25***	-0.17***	-0.07**	-0.10**	-0.08**
		(0.04)	(0.03)	(0.03)	(0.04)	(0.04)
Contrib. of trend, 2007 to 2013	-2.34	-1.10	-1.45	-1.35	-1.53	
Implied cyclical shortfall, 2014Q2	-0.12	-1.40	-1.02	-1.08	-1.02	-1.18
Observations	1836	1683	1683	1683	1224	1377
Number of states	51	51	51	51	51	51
Demographic controls	NO	NO	YES	YES	YES	YES

Weighted by state population. Standard errors clustered at the state level in parentheses.
*** denotes p<0.01, ** p<0.05, * p<0.1.

As shown in column (1) of table 3, the cyclical parameter β_0 is -0.17 when only the contemporaneous unemployment rate is included in the specification.[13] Defining the contribution of trend to be the contribution of the year fixed effects and state time trends (that is, everything but the unemployment rate), this specification implies that trend participation fell by

---

[12] For these specifications, we construct labor force participation rates, unemployment rates, and demographic controls by state-year from the CPS microdata. The covariates included in vector X are the share, by state and year, in each of 24 demographic groups defined by sex, education, and age (where the two education groups are persons with no more than a high school degree and persons with at least some college or more, and the six age groups are 16-24, 25-34, 35-44, 45-54, 55-64, and 65 and older). Estimates from specifications that excluded state-specific trends were qualitatively similar to the results shown in table 3.

[13] One caveat to the use of the unemployment rate as the indicator of the business cycle is that it might be endogenous to changes in the participation rate. To address this potential endogeneity, we also ran regressions with instrumental variables and obtained similar results. An alternative possibility would be to use (detrended) employment as a measure of business cycle. However, since (state) employment trends necessarily depend on (state) trend participation rate movements, the employment gap measures suffer from the same problem of endogeneity.

2.3 percentage points from 2007 to 2013. Defining the cyclical shortfall in the participation rate in 2014Q2 to be β_0 multiplied by the cyclical shortfall in the unemployment rate as estimated by the CBO (the difference between the actual unemployment rate and the CBO's estimate of the long-run natural rate, a gap that was about 0.7 percentage point in 2014Q2), the estimated cyclical shortfall in the participation rate from this specification is only -0.1 percentage point.

The next column adds three lags of the unemployment rate. Overall, these lags tend to be statistically significant at conventional levels, are negative in sign, and in some cases are quite large.[14] In fact, the magnitudes of the later lags (the third lag in particular) are so large as to raise questions about mis-specification, which we will return to in a moment. Nevertheless, taking this specification at face value, the implied cyclical shortfall in participation in 2014Q2 is nearly 1½ percentage points and the contribution of the trend decline in participation falls to about 1 percentage point.[15] Adding demographic controls (column 3) reduces the estimate of the cyclical shortfall somewhat and boosts the contribution of trend (for these calculations, the contribution of the demographic controls are included in the trend). Nevertheless, at 1 percentage point the current cyclical shortfall is still sizable.

Motivated by the implausibly large effect of longer lags of the unemployment rate, we next include one lag of the participation rate. Theoretically, lags of the participation rate could matter if labor force participation is a persistent state, for example, if hysteresis effects or

---

[14] The CEA (2014) report estimates similarly-specified regressions using national data and finds significant lagged effects from the unemployment gap on participation of up to 8 quarters. Moreover, the IMF (2014) report estimates from similar regressions using state-level data and finds significant lagged effects from the employment gap on participation up to 3 years.

[15] The cyclical shortfall in 2014Q2 is calculated as described for the regression of column 1, except that we also account for lags by multiplying the coefficient on each lag by the second-quarter estimate of the cyclical shortfall in unemployment (actual unemployment rate less the CBO's estimate of the natural rate) for one, two, or three years previously.

transition costs are important.[16] In this case, our finding that lags of the unemployment rate are sizable could reflect the effect of the cycle on the participation rate in previous years, rather than direct effects of lagged unemployment rates. Indeed, when we include one lag of the participation rate (column 4), the coefficients on lags of the unemployment rate are smaller and the pattern appears more plausible (earlier lags tend to be larger, and the magnitude of the third lag is more than halved).[17] Nevertheless, in this specification, the implied current cyclical shortfall in participation is about the same as the previous specification (1 percentage point), although the contribution of trend is a bit larger.[18]

Finally, we have explored the robustness of these findings to different sample periods. In column 5 we limit the sample to 1990 and later. The contribution of the trend to the post-2007 decline and the estimate of the current cyclical shortfall in participation are fairly similar to the estimates from the full sample. When we limit estimation to the pre-2007 period, the estimate of the current cyclical shortfall is again similar to previous estimates.

---

[16] See, for example, Clark and Summers (1982).

[17] We estimate these specifications using weighted least squares. However, because coefficient estimates from panel data regressions with lagged dependent variables and fixed effects may be biased (see, for instance, Judson and Owen 1999), we have experimented using the Arellano and Bond (1991) estimator. As a practical matter, this is difficult to implement for several reasons: we include a large number of right-hand side variables (including 51 state trends), we weight our variables by population, and we cluster our standard errors. Nevertheless, preliminary work using an Arellano and Bond type estimator suggest that the resulting trend and cycle point estimates are quite similar to what we present here.

[18] To estimate the cyclical shortfall implied by these regressions, we start by estimating the shortfall implied directly by the unemployment rate and its lags, as described previously. However, lags of the unemployment rate also contribute indirectly via effects on lagged participation. Since participation one year ago is also influenced by participation in the previous year (and hence, another three lags of the unemployment rate), the total cyclical contribution of the unemployment rate and its lags is an infinite series that is a function of the coefficients on the lagged participation and unemployment rates. To simplify our calculations, we approximate the cyclical shortfall by adding to the direct effect of the unemployment rate and its lags two terms that are a function of the effects of unemployment on the participation rate in the previous two years and the coefficient on lagged participation. That is, the cyclical shortfall for column 4 is: $\beta_0 \widetilde{UR}_t + \sum_{i=3} \beta_i \widetilde{UR}_{t-i} + \lambda \left(\beta_0 \widetilde{UR}_{t-1} + \sum_3 \beta_i \widetilde{UR}_{t-(i+1)} \right) + \lambda^2 \left(\beta_0 \widetilde{UR}_{t-2} + \sum_3 \beta_i \widetilde{UR}_{t-(i+2)} \right)$, where $\widetilde{UR}_t$ is the difference between the actual unemployment rate and the CBO's estimate of the natural rate for the second quarter of year t.

To summarize, our investigation of the relationship between state-level unemployment and participation rates over a multi-decade period suggests that the cyclical shortfall in the participation rate in 2014Q2 is between -0.1 percentage point (no lags of the participation or unemployment rates) and -1.0 percentage point (one lag of the participation rate and 3 lags of the unemployment rate). The estimated decline in trend participation between 2007 and 2013 is between 1¼ and 1½ percentage points when lags of the participation and unemployment rates are included. Finally, the estimate of the current cyclical shortfall is remarkably similar regardless of whether we limit our sample to earlier or later periods. In contrast to the cross-state regressions presented in the earlier section, regressions that use a longer panel of state-level data suggest that trend factors have played a much larger role in explaining recent declines in participation. Nevertheless, they also suggest that the current cyclical shortfall is sizable.

We conclude this section by cautioning that the estimated link between state-level labor force participation rates and state-level unemployment rate can be interpreted in several possible ways. First, the participation rate changes could be related to discouragement and thus likely to reverse as the economy strengthens further. Second, the recession might have merely accelerated trend declines that would have happened anyway (e.g., retirements) and hence are unlikely to reverse. Third, the recession may have caused cyclical declines in the participation rate that will eventually become permanent (e.g., retirement or disability). Fourth, it is conceivable that the correlation might be spurious, if, for example, states with a larger share of older population (and thus more subject to participation declines due to aging) are more prone to housing booms and busts, and thus more severe downturns. In this sense, empirical models that explicitly control for some of the above mentioned factors are better equipped to distinguish between trend, as we have defined it, and cycle.

V. Additional explanations for the decline in participation

Taking the results of the previous sections at face value, of the 2¾ percentage point decline in participation since 2007, aging appears to explain roughly 1¼ percentage points of the decline, while ¼ to 1 percentage point may be attributable to a weak labor market (and the lagged effect of the weak labor market over the last few years). While these results are suggestive, they do not constitute a comprehensive decomposition, and they leave many questions unanswered. For instance, they cannot inform us on the extent to which the remaining decline represents a continuation of secular declines in participation in some age groups that pre-dated the recession and would have occurred even in the absence of a recession. Indeed, the top panel of figure 4 plots age and education-specific participation rates, and shows that participation rates were falling for younger persons (16-24 years old) and prime-age individuals (24-54 years old) without a college degree for many years prior to the recession. (In contrast, there has been an ongoing upward trend in participation rates for individuals 55years and older). Nor can the previous results speak to whether the severity of the recession and subsequently slow labor market recovery may have induced atypically large responses on some margins of participation, such as retirement and disability insurance receipt, which are less likely to be reversed going forward. In this section, we speculate on the likelihood of these possibilities.

The decline in participation for teenagers and young adults

As highlighted by the bottom panel of figure 4, the labor force participation rate for 16-24 year olds has declined from about 66 percent in 2000 to roughly 55 percent in mid-2014. In fact, the decline in participation for this group has been so large that it accounts for roughly 40 percent of the downtrend in aggregate participation over this 15-year period. While this trend has been documented by a number of researchers, a cohesive explanation has remained elusive.[19]

We begin with an examination of whether an increase in schooling or schooling intensity can explain the bulk of the decline in participation for this age group. Consistent with education as an important explanation, the drop in labor force participation among youths coincides with a general rise in their school enrollment rates (figure 5).[20] For younger adults (19-24), the rise in school enrollment reflects rising college enrollment, likely in response to the historically high college earnings premium (e.g. Autor, 2014). For high school age students (16-18), rising annual average school enrollment rates mostly reflect higher schooling rates in the *summer*.[21]

Figure 5 also indicates that youths who report being enrolled in school in the CPS have lower labor force participation rates on average, suggesting that the rise in enrollment helps to explain some of the decline in participation for this age group. However, participation rates have been falling for *both* enrolled and non-enrolled individuals, indicating that rising enrollment cannot explain the entirety of the overall decline. To quantify the contribution of rising enrollment to declining participation, we construct a counterfactual participation rate by fixing

---

[19] For some earlier work on the subject, see Aaronson, Kyung-Hong, and Sullivan (2006), Morisi (2008, 2010), and Smith (2011).

[20] In these figures, enrollment is measured by the response to the CPS question: "Last week was [the respondent] attending or enrolled in a high school, college, or university? Yes if currently on holiday or seasonal vacation, no if on summer vacation." Of note, the question is phrased such that persons on summer vacation should not report themselves as being enrolled.

[21] Reported high school enrollment over traditional "school year" months (January through April, and September through December) also rose from the mid-1980s to 2013, but not by nearly as much as during summer months. From 2010-2012, on average 91 percent of 16-18 year olds report in the CPS being in school during school year months, up from about 83 percent in the mid-1980s; the comparable figures for traditional non-school year summer months are 58 percent in 2010-2012 and 19 percent in the mid-1980s. Regarding the rise in reported summer enrollment, it is unclear exactly what this represents. One possibility is that this reflects increased time spent in academic camps or other activities meant to enhance students' college resumes and improve chances of getting into college or a better college. Alternatively, it could be due to a rise in formal summer school attendance. Unfortunately, the sample size for these select months and ages from American Time Use Survey is too small to make meaningful inference, and we were unable to find comprehensive, administrative data on formal summer school enrollment.

enrollment rates at their 1985 levels and letting participation rates for enrolled and non-enrolled 16-24 year olds evolve as they did (plotted as the counterfactual participation rate in figure 6). This counterfactual suggests that rising enrollment accounted for about one-half of the decline in participation for this group over the past three decades and about one-quarter of the decline since 2000.[22] A similar exercise for 2007-2012 implies that the rise in enrollment can explain 1¼ percentage points of the 4¾ percentage point decline in participation for 16-24 year olds over this period, or about 0.2 percentage point of the decline in the aggregate participation rate.

Of the remaining 3½ percentage point decline in the youth participation rate since 2007, a simple decomposition suggests that about 2½ percentage points is attributable to the decline in participation of enrolled persons, and 1 percentage point is due to the decline in participation of non-enrolled persons.[23] Among enrollees, a portion of the decline may be attributable to increased educational intensity, such as greater time spent on homework or other extracurricular activities, which itself may have been induced by the elevated college earnings premium.[24] Indeed, according to estimates from the American Time Use Survey (which only begin in 2003), for 16-24 year olds who reported being enrolled in high school or college, the average time spent

---

[22] Unfortunately, it appears that the enrollment variable in the CPS after 2012 is not strictly comparable to that in prior years. Prior to 2013, current enrollment status was only asked for respondents up to 24 years old. After 2013, it was asked of individuals up to age 54. Coincident with this change, reported enrollment for ages 24 and younger shows a discrete jump in 2013, which we suspect may be due to changes in the way that the question was asked. For this reason, we only show enrollment rates through 2012, and our counterfactual activity only examines changes in participation through 2012.

[23] To arrive at this estimate, we decomposed the decline in participation from 2007 to 2012 into: 1) the decline attributable to falling participation for enrolled persons (the change in participation for enrolled persons multiplied by the share enrolled in 2007); 2) the decline attributable to falling participation for non-enrolled persons (the change in participation for non-enrolled persons multiplied by the share not enrolled in 2007); and 3) the decline attributable to the rise in the enrollment share (difference in participation for enrolled and non-enrolled persons in 2012 multiplied by the average change in enrollment rates from 2007 to 2012).

[24] For high school age persons, this is consistent with the findings in Ramey and Ramey (2010), which show that the amount of time spent by parents (especially college-educated parents) on activities for their children has been rising over time (particularly for older children, and in the "travel" and "activities" categories). They attribute these trends in time-use to increased competition for college admissions, leading children and parents to spend more time on college-preparatory activities.

daily on education-related activities increased by nearly 8 percent from 2003-2007 to 2008-2013 for high school students and by 15 percent for college students.

While education-related reasons (such as the rising returns to a college degree) seem likely to be an important explanation for the decline in participation of high-school and college-age individuals over the past two decades, they cannot explain the decline in participation for *non-enrolled* persons.[25] That said, the two phenomena may be related. For example, the flip side of the increased demand for college-educated workers has been a decrease in demand for some adult workers lower on the educational scale, which may have displaced them into lower-skilled sectors, thus increasing competition for jobs in the low-skilled labor market (e.g. retail sales and food service) and crowding out younger job seekers. We explore this idea more carefully in the next section. Finally, another on-going source of crowd-out may be the increasing population share of less-educated adult immigrants, as some evidence suggests that the displacement effect of immigration on the employment of younger persons is much larger than on the employment of prime-age adults (Smith, 2012).

The role of polarization in the secular decline in participation for less-educated adults

Returning to the top panel of figure 4, prime age males without a college degree have experienced a long secular decline in their participation rates, joined by prime age women without a college degree beginning in the early 2000s. These declines have been the subject of a considerable literature reaching back to the 1980s. The early literature, which focused on prime age men, identified declining labor market opportunities for low-skilled workers, manifested in stagnant real wage growth, as the likely explanation (e.g. Juhn, 1992). However, since the

---

[25] In the ATUS, non-enrolled individuals report spending very little time on education-related activities (on average, less than 5 minutes per day).

1990s, changes in labor demand have not been characterized by a monotonic increase in the demand for skilled workers, but rather by a decline in labor demand for occupations that have tended to be "middle-paying" or middle-skill jobs, and a concurrent increase in the both the share employed in higher-paying jobs (for better educated persons) and the share employed in lower-paying jobs (for less educated persons), e.g. Autor 2010.[26] Can this polarization explain the decline in labor force participation among these workers over the past decade or two?

Polarization in labor demand, driven by exogenous technological changes and globalization, seems at least a plausible candidate explanation for some of the secular decline in participation among less-educated individuals. The idea is that polarization, while increasing demand for better-educated workers, displaces some less-educated (non-college) workers who were employed in middle-type jobs. Of these, some are able to transition to high-type jobs, some transition into the lower-paying service sector (perhaps displacing lower-skilled workers), and some may temporarily or permanently drop out of the labor force, as the decline in demand for their labor pushes their offer wages below their reservation level.[27] Labor force withdrawal is likely to be most acute for less-educated adults, since they are most likely to have been employed in middle-type or lower-type jobs.[28]

---

[26] The latest research explains labor market polarization as a consequence of two factors: the decline in the cost of computing and automation technology and the increased accessibility of overseas labor and product markets (see Autor et al., 2013). While these developments appear to have directly reduced labor demand for individuals in middle-type occupations, they likely *raised* labor demand for more educated individuals and had little direct effect on labor demand for service-sector type.

[27] Displacement out of the labor force from middle-type jobs due to these forces may also have been exacerbated by the concurrent liberalization of disability insurance (DI), which lowered the costs of dropping out of the labor force by raising the likelihood of DI benefit receipt and providing more generous benefits to those on disability rolls (Autor and Duggan, 2006; Duggan and Imberman, 2009).

[28] In 1985, of those without a four-year college degree, 21 percent of prime-age males and 45 percent of prime-age females were employed in middle-type jobs. Of those with a four year college degree or more, only 11 percent of males and 28 percent of females were employed in middle-type jobs.

Panel A of figure 7 shows the share of all employed persons in the CPS who report being employed in "high-type" occupations which tend to be better paid and require more education (managerial, professional, and technical occupations), "middle-type" occupations which tend to require less education but pay reasonably well among jobs with similar educational requirements (non-managerial, non-supervisory machine operators, production workers, or office administration workers), "lower-type" occupations which tend to pay lower wages (for instance, non-managerial and non-supervisory service sector jobs in hospitality or retail), and other non-managerial, non-supervisory jobs which also tend to require less education but pay better than service sector jobs (construction, extraction and transportation occupations).[29] As has been documented in much other work, the share of persons employed in middle-type jobs has been falling, while the shares employed in low-skilled service sector jobs and jobs that tend to require a college degree have been increasing.[30] In particular, over this period, the share of prime age men without a college degree employed in middle-type jobs has fallen while the share employed in lower-type jobs has increased significantly (panel B of figure 7), and these trends have been starker than for more-educated persons (not shown).

While it is difficult to prove that polarization of labor demand *caused* a substantial portion of the observed decline in labor force participation among less-educated individuals, exploratory econometric evidence is supportive of the hypothesis. Table 4 shows results from

[29] When studying the effects of labor market polarization, researchers have tended to focus on changes in employment shares across different types of occupations. The canonical treatment of polarization divides occupations based on the tasks that the jobs primarily require, specifically whether the tasks are routine or manual, and cognitive or manual (e.g. Acemoglu and Autor, 2011). Researchers have noted that non-routine, cognitive jobs tend to require higher education and be higher paying; routine jobs tend to require less education but pay reasonably well for jobs that require less education; and non-routine manual jobs also require less education but pay less. This division roughly maps into the occupational split that we show in figure 7: High-type jobs are generally non-routine cognitive, middle-type jobs are routine, and low-type jobs are non-routine manual.

[30] These aggregate trends are somewhat contaminated by compositional shifts in the population towards higher education. Within education groups, there has been an even greater shift from middle-type to lower-type jobs, particularly for persons without a college degree, but recently even for college-educated individuals (Beaudry, Green, and Sand, 2013.)

cross-state regressions in which the dependent variable is the change in the participation rate for various demographic groups, and the right-hand side variable of interest is the change in the share of all adults in middle-type jobs, which is a proxy for the degree of polarization in the state.[31] As suggested by the theory outlined above, participation rates for less educated adults (columns 2 and 3) fell more in states with a greater decline in middle-type employment shares, and the elasticity is greater for these groups than for the participation rates for more educated adults (columns 4 and 5).[32] Nevertheless, participation rates for higher-educated persons also fell more in states that experienced greater polarization, potentially consistent with the Beaudry, Green, and Sand observation that the effects of polarization have recently begun to creep up the education distribution. Additionally, column 5 of Table 4 shows that participation of 16-24 year olds fell more in states that experienced greater polarization, consistent with the earlier discussion of the decline in participation among younger persons (i.e. rising college wage premium leading to substitution towards more schooling and crowd-out by adults in the low-wage service sector).

Admittedly, this evidence is indirect. Nevertheless, polarization in labor demand is one of the most striking developments in the labor market over the last few decades, and it would be surprising if such a pervasive change has not left a noticeable imprint on aspects of labor supply, including participation rate trends.

---

[31] There is a reasonable amount of variation across states in this measure. For example, between 1985/1989 and 2009/2013, the share of persons employed in middle-type jobs was roughly flat in South Dakota and North Dakota, and fell by over 10 percentage points in South Carolina, Georgia, Massachusetts, Connecticut, and Tennessee.

[32] Further supporting this idea, and following the logic of Autor and Dorn, 2013, states for which employment was most concentrated in middle-type jobs in 1980—and which were therefore set to benefit most from subsequent developments in technology and globalization—experienced the greatest declines both in middle-type employment and in participation rates for less-educated, prime-age adults.

Table 4: Relationship Between Change in Participation and Change in the Share Employed in Mid-Type Jobs (1985-1989 to 2009-2014 Averages)

| | 25-54, less ed. | | 25-54, more ed. | | |
	Male	Female	Male	Female	16-24
Change in share employed in middle-type jobs, pp.	0.34 (0.16)	0.47 (0.17)	0.14 (0.07)	0.33 (0.15)	0.71 (0.16)

Note: Table show estimates of the cross-state relationship between the change in the average share of prime-age adults employed in middle-type jobs (1985-1989 average to 2009-2014 average) and the change in the LFPR for select groups. Each column represents a separate regression, where the LHS variable is the change in the LFPR for the listed group. The table gives the coefficient on the change in the share in middle-type jobs, with standard errors are in parentheses. Middle-type jobs are defined as non-managerial office administration or production jobs. Estimates are authors' calculations from CPS microdata.

A final thought on the topic concerns the relationship between polarization and the cyclical response of participation in the wake of the financial crisis. Obviously, polarization is a long-term phenomenon. That said, some research suggests that it accelerates during recessions (Jaimovich and Siu, 2012). Consistent with this phenomenon, the participation rate for less-educated prime-age men has also exhibited a stair-step pattern, discretely falling during the recession and failing to recover thereafter (figure 4, panel B). Whether this pattern represents an actual acceleration of the process or just the reemergence of the trend during a cyclical downturn, the result is the same – polarization does not unwind as the economy expands. Thus to the extent that polarization explains the decline in labor force participation, we would not expect to see an increase in participation among these workers as the labor market improves.

This discussion is not meant to preclude other possible explanations for the decline in participation among prime age workers, prime age men in particular. One alternative is the increase in labor market opportunities for females, which could have resulted in a shift in the relative gender balance for providing household income. However, this theory has to contend with the declining participation of less-educated women since the early 2000s.

The role of retirements and disability

As shown in Section III, the changing age distribution of the population can account for nearly half of the decline in the labor force participation rate since 2007. In this section we examine two of the age-related factors contributing to declining participation rate in recent years: retirement and disability.

Retirement

Assessing the role of retirements for labor force participation since the start of the Great Recession is particularly challenging for several reasons. First, the leading-edge of the baby-boom generation reached age 62 – the minimum age to receive Social Security retirement benefits – in 2008, concomitantly with the onset of the recession. Thus, we would have expected an upswing in retirements to begin even absent the recession, which complicates the attempt to distinguish structural and cyclical factors. Moreover, while the recession likely affected many retirement decisions, the direction of the effect is uncertain. On the one hand, staggering job losses during the recession and a subsequent lack of employment opportunities undoubtedly led some individuals to enter retirement sooner than planned. On the other hand, the financial crisis, with its associated losses in housing and stock market wealth, wreaked havoc on household balance sheets, likely causing some individuals to delay their retirement.

Evidence for the expected increase in retirements associated with the aging of the baby-boom cohort is clear. As can be seen in panel A of figure 8, and as has been reported elsewhere, the share of the working-age population reporting as retired in the CPS has risen by over a percentage point since 2007.[33] However, the dashed line, which holds the fraction retired at each age constant at their 2007 levels, illustrates that actual retirements during the recession and early recovery have lagged what would have been predicted by the changing age composition alone. Instead, within-age retirement rates declined modestly between 2007 and 2011, offsetting much of the effect of aging during this period.[34]

However, as can be seen in panel B of figure 8, within-age retirement rates actually started declining around the late 1990s, likely due to a combination of institutional changes in social security and pension plans, increasing levels of education among older individuals, and longer lifespans.[35] There is no obvious impact of the Great Recession and its aftermath on within-group retirement rates, and thus no clear evidence in favor of a dominant effect from either increased early retirements due to discouragement or deferred retirements due to lower-than-expected asset accumulation.[36] Looking again at panel A, since 2012 – which is also the year when the first baby boomers reached full retirement age – actual retirements as measured by the CPS have risen broadly in line with predicted retirements on the basis of the changing age composition, with the share of retirees in the US population rising about 0.3 percentage point per year.

While the CPS data are a particularly useful source of data on retirement for our purposes, since they come from the same survey as the published labor force participation rate,

[33] Fujita (2014) also noted that CPS retirements have edged up over recent years, but he has not investigated whether this rise is consistent with aging and institutional changes as we do here.
[34] A recent study by Helman et al. (2014) finds that the share of retirees saying that they retired earlier than planned rose from just under 40 percent in the years prior to the recession to closer to 50 percent during the recession and in the years since. The share reporting retiring later than expected also edged up slightly. Gorodnichenko, Song, and Stolyarov (2013) find that over time white men have increasingly reacted to recessions by retiring. While this evidence is suggestive of a behavioral response to the recent business cycle, it is difficult to see in the aggregate data from the CPS.
[35] See Mastrobuoni (2009) and Blau and Goodstein (2010).
[36] Bosworth and Burtless (2010) also find economically modest effects of the Great Recession on the labor force participation rate of older workers.

they are not the only source of data on the issue. Panel C of figure 8 plots Social Security retirement recipients as a percent of the working-age population; this measure also shows a sharp upturn in retirements in recent years. In contrast to the CPS series, however, Social Security retirements started to turn up during the recession. One possible interpretation of these patterns is that some individuals who lost their jobs began to collect Social Security retirement benefits during the recession (perhaps before their full retirement age) but nevertheless remained in the labor force to search for a new job.[37]

Disability

Turning to disability, the thin line in panel A of figure 9 depicts CPS self-reported nonparticipation in the labor force due to disability. Nonparticipation due to disability as a percent of the US working-age population has been edging up by about 0.1 percentage point annually over the past decade or so, which appears to be mostly due to structural factors, with only a little evidence of cyclicality.[38]

While the CPS definition of disability does not depend on the receipt of SSDI and there is a difference in the levels of the CPS data and the administrative data on the receipt of SSDI benefits (the thick black line), their trajectories track each other reasonably well.[39] Focusing on the administrative data, once we account for the increase in SSDI receipts resulting from the rise in the social security full retirement age from 65 to 66 by concentrating on persons 64 and under, there is only scant indication of a cyclical increase in benefit receipt.

---

[37] The levels of these series are not strictly comparable because the CPS measure includes younger retirees who are not yet eligible to receive Social Security benefits.

[38] For a further analysis of factors behind the rising disability, see Autor and Duggan (2003), Duggan and Imberman (2009), and Autor (2011).

[39] As pointed out in Fujita (2014), p. 3, although CPS disability is self-reported and is not related to the receipt of SSDI, it is nonetheless a fairly strict definition.

That said, applications for Social Security disability insurance benefits (the dotted line) did step up during the recession and only began to ease in late 2012. This increase in applications alone could have resulted in a decrease in labor force participation, as applicants often view themselves as effectively disqualified from working (Autor, 2011). However, we would expect any such effect to be reflected in the CPS disability measure, which as mentioned, does not seem to have risen more quickly after 2008 than before. To the contrary, disability in the CPS seems to have continued to rise in recent years even as applications and actual benefit receipts have stabilized, a discrepancy for which we have no ready explanation.

Taken together, the increase in retirements and disability can account for a large portion of the rise since the recession in the share of individuals who are out of the labor market and don't want a job. However, the available evidence suggests that these increases are primarily continuations of longer-term trends and so have largely been driven by structural influences. We will discuss the future prospects for a cyclical movement of people from retirement and disability back into the labor force in section VII. But here we finish by noting that once we account for retirement and disability, there would seem to be only a little room for a cyclical recovery among other nonparticipants who say they do not want a job. This is illustrated in panel B of figure 9, which plots the cumulative change since 1995 in the share of the 16-and-over population reporting themselves out of the labor force and not wanting a job. As can be seen, this series turns up sharply after the end of the Great Recession, and then rises fairly steeply in the recovery. However, once we eliminate retirees, the series rises more slowly, and once we also eliminate those identifying themselves as out of the labor force due to disability, the series appears nearly flat, accounting for perhaps a ½ percentage point decrease in the participation rate since the recession – a not unusual movement, for instance, compared to the increase in nonparticipation in the years after the much smaller recession in the early 2000's.

VI. Declining participation through the lens of a model: Updating the model from the 2006 Brookings paper

While the analyses above go a long way towards quantifying the extent that aging, the business cycle, and an assortment of other factors can explain recent declines in participation, this factor-by-factor approach is limited in its ability to decompose the aggregate decline into cyclical and structural components in a clean, integrated and consistent fashion. Also, outside of the contributions of aging and the cycle, it is difficult to use these analyses to project the path of aggregate labor force participation over the next decade. In this section, we turn to an alternative, but complementary, approach based on an updated version of the model introduced in Aaronson and others (2006).

Description of the model

In this cohort-based, demographically disaggregated model, we combine the changing age distribution with various factors explaining within-age changes in participation. We refer the reader to the earlier Brookings paper for a general description of the model and its motivation.[40] However, we lay out the model briefly here, as the specification has changed significantly between 2006 and now.[41]

---

[40] In addition to the earlier Brookings Paper, see Fallick and Pingle (2007).
[41] Several of the changes adopted improvements introduced by Balleer et al. (2009). See also Balleer et al. (2014), Benito and Bunn (2011), Kawata and Naganuma (2010), and Duval-Hernández and Romano (2009).

Form and estimation

The model has the form

$$\log\left(\frac{lfpr_{a,t,s}}{1 - lfpr_{a,t,s}}\right) = A_{a,s} + K_{t-a,s} + X_{a,t,s}\lambda_{a,s} + \varepsilon_{a,t,s}$$

where lfpr $=$ the seasonally adjusted labor force participation rate expressed as a fraction,

a $=$ age (in single years), 16 to 79[42]

t $=$ calendar time (in quarters)

s $=$ sex

A $=$ an age-and-sex-specific constant, i.e., an "age effect"

K $=$ a birth-year-and-sex-specific constant, i.e., a "cohort effect" [43]

X $=$ a vector of variables that may vary by age, time and/or sex

λ $=$ a vector of coefficients, which generally vary by both age and sex. Some coefficients are constrained to be zero for some age-sex groups.

ε $=$ an i.i.d. error term.

We draw the data on participation rates by age and sex from the micro CPS files, adjust the raw series to account for changes in the survey and changes in the population controls, and seasonally adjust them.[44] For these reasons, the aggregate participation rates implied by these age/sex-specific participation rates differ slightly from the published aggregate rates.

---

[42] We do not model the participation rates of persons 80 years or older, because of the small sample size and very low participation rates of this group. In summing to an aggregate participation rate, we treat the rate of the 80+ group as always at trend.

[43] Because birth dates are spread throughout the calendar year, current year minus reported age is not a perfect measure of birth year, nor should the cohort effects jump sharply from one birth year to the next. Therefore in the estimation each cohort effect K contributes in a weighted fashion to the equations for adjacent years.

[44] We use second-stage final weights of the individual data used to construct the participation rates because composite weights not being available for the earlier years of our sample. In addition, we apply the seasonal factors provided by the BLS for various age groups to seasonally adjust the data; each age is assigned the seasonal factor for the smallest containing age group for which the BLS provides a seasonal factor.

We include ten variables in the vector X:

A. The aggregate *unemployment rate gap*, divided into positive and negative components in order to allow for asymmetric responses to tight and loose labor markets. We use the long-term natural rate estimated by the CBO to define the unemployment rate gap. Our baseline specification includes the contemporaneous gaps and lags at 4-, 8-, and 12- quarters. We have also estimated the model using only the contemporaneous unemployment rate gap and with other lag lengths; all yield similar results.[45]

B. The aggregate *personal bankruptcy rate*, as a percent of the population. In principal, household wealth should influence participation decisions, most notably for retirement. However, these effects are difficult to identify in aggregate data, possibly because holdings of wealth are so skewed. The personal bankruptcy rate is intended to represent changes in household wealth at the most relevant parts of its distribution.

C. The percent of each age-sex group with a *college degree*. Participation rates differ significantly by education, which is typically attributed to a combination of higher returns to market work and, especially at older ages, the lower physical demands usually associated with occupations requiring greater education. Although we include only college attainment explicitly, this variable is intended to represent the patterns in educational attainment in general, which are highly correlated over time with college attainment. We tabulate this variable from the micro CPS data and include these demographically disaggregated college degree rates for ages 27 and over for both sexes.

D. *Life expectancy* conditional on survival to each age, 55 to 79. Because mortality and morbidity at older ages tend to improve together, this variable is intended to represent changes in

---

[45] All variables except these two unemployment rate gaps are normalized to have mean zero and variance one, in order to facilitate comparisons across coefficients.

both.[46] Higher life expectancy should increase participation by raising the level of assets

necessary to finance retirement at any given age. Lower morbidity – better health at higher ages

– should be associated with a lower disutility of participation.

E. The *Social Security "pay-out rate."* This is the average fraction of the Primary Insurance

Amount (PIA) a person would receive if he or she were to retire at a particular age.[47] For

persons below the statutory normal retirement age, a higher value implies a smaller penalty for

retiring early. For older persons, a higher value of the variable implies a greater reward for

delaying retirement.

F. *Marriage and young children.* The associations between labor force participation and the

presence of young children appear to vary by marital status, and vice-versa. We therefore

include three variables to capture this interaction, at least crudely: the percentage of women who

are married with a child less than 6 years old, the percentage of women who are not married with

a child less than 6 years old, and the percentage of women married without a child less than 6

years old.[48]

G. The ratio of the effective *minimum wage*, adjusted to account for state-level minimum

wages that are above the federal level, relative to average hourly earnings.[49]

H. The ratio of the *median hourly wage rate for ages 16-19* to the median hourly wage rate

for ages 25 plus.[50] This variable is intended to reflect movements in the relative demand for

teenagers, perhaps due to the factors discussed above in section V.

---

[46] We use sex-specific estimates of life expectancy from the Census Bureau. We include this variable for ages 55 and over of both sexes.

[47] We include the pay-out rate for ages 62-79 of both sexes.

[48] We tabulate these percentages, by age, from the micro CPS data. We include the first two of these variables for women ages 18-45, and the third for women ages 18-61. Very few women over the age of 45 have children less than 6 years old, so for the 46-plus ages the third variable acts simply as percent married.

[49] Specifically, we define the ratio of the minimum wage as a population-weighted average of federal and state minimums, to average hourly earnings. We include this variable for ages 16 to 19 for both sexes.

I. The ratio of summer to non-summer *school enrollment rates*, by age and sex, among teenagers. This variable represents the expansion of schooling more generally since the mid-1990s, which, as noted above, has mainly occurred in the summer months. [51]

J. The number of *Social Security Disability Insurance* recipients, by age and sex.[52]

In what follows, we treat the unemployment rate gap (including lags) as a measure of labor market strength or weakness and the personal bankruptcy rate variable as an indicator of household balance sheets, which is also influenced by aggregate economic conditions.[53] We treat these two variables as constituting the cyclical component of the participation rate. All of the other variables, as well as the age and cohort effects, we treat as elements of the trend in participation. As noted earlier, however, the line between cycle and trend is not always clear and bright, as several of the right-hand side variables may be influenced by the business cycle to some extent. We will attempt to quantify the extent of this possible misattribution below.

In general, this model attempts to capture, in a parsimonious manner, many of the factors that we touched upon earlier in the paper. The age effects should capture the contribution of the

---

[50] We tabulate this variable from micro CPS data at the annual frequency, and smooth it using an HP filter. We include this variable for ages 16 to 19 for both sexes.

[51] Using this ratio abstracts from some of the noise in quarterly enrollment rates. We tabulate this from micro CPS data. We include this variable for ages 16 to 19 for both sexes. However, we enter this variable in a different fashion than the others. (See the footnote below.)

[52] By age and sex, we divide the number of SSA disability recipients in current payment status by the population for that age and sex computed from micro CPS data. We include this variable for ages 30 to 64 for both sexes. Because recipients rarely stop receiving Social Security disability payments until they "age out" or die, we essentially treat recipiency as a predetermined variable with respect to labor force participation.

[53] The unemployment rate gap is not a perfect measure of the cycle for our purposes. Most importantly, if the unemployment rate is artificially low due to a cyclically-depressed participation rate, then the model-implied cyclical participation rate component will be biased. Our analysis above suggests that this is probably not a major problem, but it remains an area of concern. One could use alternative cyclical indicators, such as the capacity utilization index, output gap or (detrended) non-farm payrolls. However, these indicators have their own flaws, which are arguably as significant as those of the unemployment rate. The capacity utilization index only measures utilization for the manufacturing sector, not the whole economy. The output gap depends on potential output, which is unobserved and has been subject to substantial uncertainty and considerable revisions since the Great Recession. Moreover, any estimate of potential output that is built up from fundamentals will depend on estimates of trend participation (and hence will be endogenous). Finally, measures of payroll growth must necessarily be de-trended to account for changes in labor supply, and thus will also depend on an estimate for trend participation.

aging of the population. The asymmetric unemployment rate gap should capture cyclical effects. The additional right-hand side variables are included to account for some of the additional considerations discussed previously, such as retirement (proxied by our variables for life expectancy, Social Security generosity, and age effects in general), disability (proxied by the number of SSDI recipients), trends in school enrollment (proxied by the ratio of summer to non-summer enrollment), and possibly polarization.[54]

The model is estimated by least squares as a panel of 128 equations with cross-equation restrictions: one equation for each age/sex combination with the cohort effect for a given birth cohort and sex assumed to be constant across equations.[55] The coefficients on the right-hand-side variables may vary freely across age/sex combinations except for the many cases where they are constrained to be zero as noted above.[56][57]

As is well known, age, cohort, and time effects are not separately identified, and a tractable model requires choices to be made. The cohort and age effects are identified (with the cohort effects for 1975 normalized to zero) in our model because we assume that there are no time effects that are not captured by the RHS variables. The earlier Brookings paper and Fallick and Pingle (2007) argued that the cohort dimension is historically both important and

---

[54] The model likely captures some of the effects of polarization indirectly through the inclusion of right-hand side variables that are affected by polarization or correlated with its effects, such disability insurance take-up and the college share. However, it is unlikely that these variables capture the full impact of polarization, and if so, then the effect of labor market polarization on participation may be partly absorbed by the cohort effects, creating a sort of "endpoint" bias for more recent cohorts.

[55] Each age-sex-period observation is weighted based on the corresponding sample size and the value of the participation rate, under the assumption that any error in the result will be proportional to the associated log-odds transformed binomial variance for the given participation rate value.

[56] Because there are no constraints that cross sexes, the system is effectively estimated separately for men and for women.

[57] The estimated contributions to the recent decline in participation are similar when the coefficients are constrained to be constant within age groups.

meaningful, and that, therefore, restricting the time dimension to elucidate the cohort dimension was worthwhile.

This is especially true for women. As Durand (1948) observed, "As they grew older, each successive generation of women seems to have retained the greater propensity to be in the labor force which it developed in early adulthood, and so the higher percentages of labor force members have gradually been transmitted throughout the age groups from the late 20's to the early 60's." This can be seen in figure 10, which shows the participation rates for three age groups of women (35-44, 45-54, and 55-64).[58] The horizontal axis shows the birth year for the middle age of the group. In this way, each birth cohort is vertically aligned with itself at different ages. The importance of the cohort dimension can be seen in the inflection points, which occur within each age group at approximately the same birth cohorts. The apparent importance of differences in the participation rates of successive cohorts means that the evolution of the aggregate participation rate ought to be at least partly predictable. Ideally, of course, one would like to model all of the economic, technological, and social factors that led to these "greater propensity[ies] … developed in early adulthood", but that has so far not proved possible.[59]

Moreover, when it comes to the projections we show in section VII, restricting the time dimension to observables allows us to make reasonable, or at least clearly defined, assumptions about how the various factors represented by the RHS variables will evolve. We recognize that any time-varying influences not captured by the included RHS variables may contaminate the

---

[58] We use age groups because the data for the figure go back farther than data for individual ages are available.

[59] The pattern for men is less indicative of a cohort, as opposed to time, structure for the model.

cohort effects, causing the projections from the model, which propagate the cohort effects through the age distribution over time, to suffer accordingly.

Recent cohorts

Estimates of the cohort effects for cohorts that appear for only a few years at the beginning or end of our sample period are likely to suffer from endpoint bias if estimated as part of the system. Most importantly, the cohort effects for those born between 1992 and 1998 would currently be estimated using only data since the onset of the Great Recession. Not only might this give a misleading impression of how much of the recent movements in participation are trend as opposed to cycle, but because the cohort effects are assumed to persist for a lifetime, this bias could prejudice the model's predictions for future years. To mitigate this problem, we estimate the model excluding the first and last 10 cohorts from the data, for estimation of both their cohort effects and the coefficients on the right-hand side variables. The cohort effects for these cohorts are then linearly extrapolated from the adjoining 10 cohort effects.[60] This is one of the changes from the 2006 model, in which we included these cohort effects in the estimation but constrained them to evolve slowly.

Model estimates

We estimated the model on quarterly data over the period 1976:Q1 to 2014:Q2. Figure 11 shows the estimates from the baseline model.[61] The solid line in the figure shows our

---

[60] This approach leaves us unable to estimate in a satisfactory fashion the coefficients for the enrollment variable described above, for which the main variation occurs relatively recently. As a result, we omit the enrollment rate from the main procedure, regress the residuals for teenagers from the model on the enrollment variable in a second stage, and use the coefficients from this second-stage regression to recalculate the fitted values for teenagers.
[61] As noted above, our baseline specification includes lags of the two unemployment rate gap variables at 4-, 8- and 12- quarters. This choice was based on consideration of standard statistical criteria, which do not provide a definitive answer, and comparability with others' work, such as the recent report from the Council of Economic

calculated value for the actual labor force participation rate.[62] The dotted line shows the fitted

values from the model. For the most part, the model tracks the actual rate reasonably closely.

The dashed line shows the model's estimate of the trend participation rate, which, as noted

above, we define as the fitted values with the unemployment gap and the detrended personal

bankruptcy rate set to zero. The difference between the fitted and trend values is the model's

estimate of the aggregate cyclical response of the participation rate, which is shown separately in

figure 12.

According to the model's estimates, the trend participation rate fell 2.1 percentage points

between 2007:Q4 (at which point the participation rate was a little above trend) and 2014:Q2,

accounting for three-quarters of the total decline of 2.8 percentage points in the aggregate

participation rate over this period. As of 2014:Q2, the model estimates that continued weakness

in the labor market was holding the participation rate down by 0.2 percentage point, with the

currently low bankruptcy rate contributing a bit more, for a total cyclical response of

0.3 percentage point; in addition, the participation rate was 0.3 percentage point lower than the

model could explain.[63] (Of course, by construction the model cannot capture any change in the

cyclical sensitivity of participation that may have been present in the recent episode, a point to

which we will return below.) Compared to our analysis in section IV, the model estimate of the

current cyclical element is about ¼ percentage point smaller than a strict read of the increase in

---

Advisers, and the panel regressions in section IV. Results using no lags, fewer lags, or adding a 16-quarter lags are
quite similar to the baseline.
[62] As noted above, these rates differ slightly from the published rates.
[63] One may be surprised that the model does not indicate a larger cyclical decline in the depths of the Great
Recession than during, say, the 1990s recession. This is because the large increase in the personal bankruptcy rate
during the Great Recession, and the more general deterioration in household balance sheets that this presumably
indicates, worked to hold the participation rate up by inducing some affected individuals to remain in the labor
force; we classify this as a cyclical response.

- 44 -

the number of discouraged workers would suggest, and ¾ percentage point smaller than implied

by the comparable lag structure in our panel data analysis.

The decline in the aggregate trend combines the changing age distribution of the

population with disparate movements in age/sex-specific trends (which include the influence of

the cohort effects). Figure 13 summarizes these trends for several broad age/sex groups, the

general tenor of which have been well-recognized elsewhere. Participation rates for teenagers

and young adults have been trending downward for some time, with the downtrend for teenagers

(not shown separately) being particularly steep. Rates for prime-aged men have continued their

long and gradual downward trend, joined relatively recently by prime-aged women, whose

marked increase in participation ended around 1990.[64] In contrast, participation rates for older

persons have been rising since the mid-1990s. These age-specific trends combine with the

changes in the age distribution to produce the overall downward aggregate trend.[65]

We are comfortable attributing some of these age-specific trends to particular explanatory

variables. However, some of the variables in the model are highly correlated with each other,

most notably fairly monotonic variables like education levels and longevity, so the model's

attributions should be interpreted with caution. Moreover, as noted above, we intended some

variables to represent a broader set of related factors. For example, we included conditional life

expectancy in the model but assume that increases in life expectancy represent declines in age-

specific morbidity as well.

---

[64] Indeed, it may be fair to say that as women have come to resemble men along a number of labor market
dimensions, such as work experience, women have also come to join men's general downtrend in participation.
[65] Note that the model estimates trends for single-year ages. For purposes of illustration, we aggregated these into
broad age groups. Because the aggregation uses contemporaneous population shares, changes in the age
distributions within groups affect the group trends. This is particularly important for the 55 and older group. The
analysis below is based on the single-year age trends.

That said, looking over the longer sweep of the past four decades, the model attributes a large part of the rapid increase in prime-aged women's participation rates through around 1990 to an increase in the share of women who are unmarried or without young children and to rising educational attainment, counteracted to some extent by increases in disability. However, it leaves some of the increase to be accounted for by changes in cohort-specific proclivities to participate, which may reflect changes in such diverse elements as societal attitudes, workplace technologies, and reproductive technologies, to the extent that these are not already reflected in the right-hand side variables. Meanwhile, the model attributes some of the long-standing decline in male participation in this age group to an increase in disability rolls, but leaves the bulk of the downtrend to be "explained" by the cohort effects. The cohort effects are not much of an explanation, of course; they are more of a description. We suspect that the downtrend in cohort effects reflects diverse factors such as increased availability of other sources of income (such as transfer programs and labor income from other members of their households), and changes in the structure of labor demand (e.g., deindustrialization and polarization) that were unfavorable to many prime-aged men. In future work we will attempt to quantify some of these factors.

Among persons of both sexes aged 55 and up, the range for which the option of retirement is most salient, the model attributes much of the marked increase in participation rates since the mid-1990s to a number of factors, including changes to Social Security rules and increased levels of education, but the largest contributor is the increasing life expectancy of men. The entrance into this age group of female cohorts with greater attachment to the labor force also contributed, on net, over this period. This rising contribution of cohort effects is estimated to have stopped around 2010.

Participation rates for teenagers and young adults have been falling since about 1990. The model attributes the trend decline primarily to falling cohort effects, reinforced to a small extent by increasing school enrollment among teens and counteracted to some extent by changes in fertility and marriage patterns.[66] The model clearly has the greatest difficulty explaining the behavior of this group.

What of the model's interpretation of the changes since 2007? For the most part, the model attributes this decline to the same factors that have been at work over the previous two decades: A changing age distribution, falling cohort effects, rising disability rolls, and a net cyclical weakening have pushed participation down more than changing patterns of marriage and fertility and increases in education and life expectancy have pushed them up (table 5).[67] The steepening of the downtrend over this period is mainly a function of the changing age distribution, as more of the large baby-boom cohort has moved farther into the age range in which the largest drop-offs in participation rates are observed, although there is also some steepening of the decline in cohort effects, especially among prime-aged women.

---

[66] As noted above, the model does not include the school enrollment variable for young adults.

[67] Note that the contribution of the cycle to the change in the table is larger (in magnitude) than the 0.2 percentage point cited earlier because the unemployment rate was still below the natural rate in the fourth quarter of 2007.

Table 5: Contributions to the Change in LFPR, 2007:Q4 to 2014:Q2
(Percentage Points)

Source	Contribution
Age Distribution	-1.3
Cohort Effects	-1.7
Unemployment Rate Gap	-0.3
Bankruptcy Rate	-0.2
Percent with College Degree	+0.2
Life Expectancy	+0.3
Social Security Pay-Out Rate	+0.1
Marriage x young children	+0.8
Minimum Wage	0.0
Teenage Wage Ratio	0.0
Summer Enrollment Ratio	0.0
Disability Insurance	-0.5
Model Residual	-0.2

Note that the combined contribution of the elements that may be described as demographic – the age distribution, marriage x fertility, the two education variables, and life expectancy – sum to near zero over this period. However, as will become important in section VII, while we can be confident about how the age distribution will roughly evolve from this point forward, whether the other demographic variables will continue to move in an offsetting direction is more speculative.

Econometric studies have traditionally found that the aggregate participation rate varies little (about its trend) over the business cycle. With a glance at the movements around recessions and recoveries in figure 11, it should come as no surprise that our model finds a similarly small amount of cyclicality in the aggregate. By the model's estimates, a sustained 1 percentage point increase in the unemployment rate, all else equal, currently would be expected to reduce the participation rate by something on the order of 0.2 percentage point.

As noted above, some of the RHS variables in the model may themselves vary with the state of labor demand, and it is possible that the model does an inadequate job of attributing this indirect influence to the unemployment rate. In order to gain a sense of the potential size of any misattribution, we attempted to isolate the components of the suspect variables – bankruptcy, college attainment, marriage x young children, teenage/adult wage ratio, summer/nonsummer enrollment, and SSDI recipiency – orthogonal to the cyclical state of the labor market by regressing them on the unemployment rate variables. We then replaced these variables in the model with the residuals from these regressions. The resulting version of the model would attribute an additional 0.3 percentage point of the decline in aggregate participation since 2007 to labor market weakness, by increasing the estimated contribution of labor market strength in 2007.

Robustness tests

Given the severity of the Great Recession and the drawn-out nature of the recovery, one may suspect that the cyclical sensitivity of participation during this cycle to have been greater than has been typical historically. Of course, no time-series model could reliably identify a change in the cyclical coefficients in a single episode, and there is no indication in the model's residuals of nonlinearities with respect to the severity of a downturn in previous recessions. However, of particular concern in our model is that the presence of "excess cyclicality" in the past 7 years may influence the estimated cohort effects, especially for those cohorts with relatively few years in the data so far.

As described above, we attempted to mitigate any possible endpoint biases by estimating cohort effects only for cohorts with at least 10 years of available data and extrapolating cohort effects for the remaining cohorts. Given the length of the current period of labor market weakness, perhaps this is not adequate. There is a trade-off, of course, between limiting endpoint bias by reducing the number of cohorts included in the estimation and limiting the currency of the information used to estimate the model, and the proper balance is difficult to know. We explored the robustness of the model's estimates to issues of endpoint bias in the cohort effects in two ways.

First, we varied the number of cohorts whose effects are extrapolated by varying the minimum number of years of data a cohort has to have available in order to be included in the estimation. It turns out that the estimated degree of cyclicality is not sensitive to varying the number of cohorts estimated. (The variation in the estimated cyclical departure from trend in 2014:Q2, for example, amounts to well less than 0.1 percentage point.) In contrast, the estimated trends were sensitive to this choice, mostly, although not exclusively, from variation in the estimated cohort effects. Figure 14 shows the (model-data-consistent) actual participation rate and the trend participation rates from versions of the model that extrapolate differing numbers of cohorts. Reducing the number of cohorts extrapolated from the baseline model's 10 makes little difference. However, as we increase the number of cohorts extrapolated, the estimated downward trend becomes less steep, and as a result, more of the decline in participation over the past ten years is left unexplained by the model. One can see this more easily in figure 15, which shows the residuals from the model over the current cycle. That said, the elimination of so many cohorts from the estimation risks missing important information in the behavior of those born more than 25 years before the recession began—in particular much of the steep decline in the participation of young people that well-preceded the recession.

Second, we kept the number of extrapolated cohorts constant at 10, but varied the estimation period. In this way, we can remove the Great Recession and its aftermath from the estimation completely. Of course, endpoint bias in this dimension can work in either direction.

For example, if the housing boom of the mid-2000s pushed the participation rates of some groups above their trend, as might be suggested by Charles, Hurst, and Notowidigdo (2013), then ending the estimation with 2007 may bias the model's trend upward. We tried ending estimation in each of 2005:Q2, 2007:Q2, 2009:Q2, and 2010:Q2, in addition to the baseline of 2014:Q2.

As shown in figure 16, the model's estimated trend falls less steeply as we move the end date of estimation earlier, regardless of whether doing so ends the estimation in a period with a stronger or weaker labor market.[68] As a result, as when we reduced the number of cohorts included in the estimation (i.e., increased the number of cohorts extrapolated), reducing the number of years used in the estimation causes the fit of the model over the post-crisis period to deteriorate and leaves more of the net decline in participation unexplained.

As with the first exercise, the model's estimate of the sensitivity of the aggregate participation rate to the unemployment rate varies little as the end date of estimation changes. However, the same is not true for the bankruptcy rate. Without the Great Recession in the estimation period, the coefficients on the bankruptcy rate are small and, when aggregated, negative. Evidently, and not surprisingly given the relatively small and transient previous movements in the (detrended) bankruptcy rate, the large losses of the recent housing bust and financial crisis provide the main identification of these coefficients in the baseline estimation.

---

[68] The current model estimated through 2005 produces a noticeably smaller decline in the trend since 2007 than was projected by the model in the 2006 Brookings Paper. As noted above, we made several changes to the current version of the model relative to the 2006 vintage. In addition, the current exercise uses the actual values of the right-hand side variables for the post-2005 period, whereas the 2006 paper held many of these variables constant over what was then the projection period. Of these, the most important for explaining this discrepancy appear to be a new method of extrapolation of cohort effects for the youngest cohorts and the use of actual post-2005 values for the right-hand side variables.

VII. Future Prospects

To summarize the results so far, the model attributes three-quarters of the decline in the labor force participation rate since 2007 to demographics and other factors mostly captured by the cohort effects. We have argued that the latter probably represent factors such as labor market polarization and rising disability rolls, which are likely to be structural. This raises the question of how much scope there is for participation to recover as the economy improves. As the unemployment rate continues to move toward its natural rate, we would expect the participation rate to move back toward its trend (which could simply entail the participation rate moving sideways or declining less quickly relative to its downward trend). However, the line between being out of the labor force and unemployed can be fluid, and it is possible that some people who we might consider to have dropped out of the labor force for structural, rather than cyclical, reasons could re-enter if appropriate opportunities arose. Indeed, the participation rate was above the model's estimate of the trend just prior to the financial crisis, when the unemployment rate was low. Therefore in this section we discuss some ways to think about likely future outcomes.

As noted above, the participation rate on aggregate has not exhibited sizable cyclical fluctuations in the past. According to our model, at current levels, a 1 percentage point decrease in the unemployment rate, taken alone, would result in about a 0.2 percentage point increase in the participation rate (although our panel regressions suggest an effect up to twice as large, depending on our specification). While labor force participation among certain groups, notably teenagers, does move more closely with the business cycle, these groups constitute a relatively small share of the population, and therefore impart only modest cyclicality to the aggregate participation rate. If the unemployment rate were to continue to decline at its pace of recent years of about ¼ percentage point per quarter, it would reach the CBO's estimate of the long-term natural rate of unemployment in 2015:Q1. Under this assumption, and given the lags in the baseline specification, the model would predict the participation rate to fall to its trend level about a year later (see below).

Might we see a greater cyclical rebound than usual?

However, the severity of the recent recession raises the question of whether the historical degree of cyclical sensitivity of participation is a good guide to the current situation. In answering this question, it helps to examine the underlying dynamics of labor force participation as illustrated by the gross monthly labor force flows in the CPS.[69] As can be seen in figure 17, it turns out that the nearly acyclical nature of the participation rate is the product of two opposing factors. The monthly rate at which individuals enter the labor force for employment (NE flow) declines as the unemployment rate increases (panel A), no doubt as a result of reduced employment opportunities.[70] But at the same time, monthly transitions from outside of the labor force into unemployment (NU flow) increase (panel B). It may be that the increase in NU flows is also related to poor labor market demand, as individuals who ordinarily would have moved from out of the labor force into a job (such as recent graduates) endure a spell of unemployment when opportunities are poor.[71] Whatever the explanation, combining the two flows results in a pattern of overall flows from not in the labor force into the labor force that is indeed acyclical

---

[69] This analysis uses the monthly flows published by the BLS, which have been seasonally adjusted and raked to be consistent with the published levels.

[70] A similar chart has been plotted by Matthew O'Brien in *The Atlantic*. See "The Fed Absolutely Shouldn't Give Up on the Long-Term Unemployed," March 12, 2014.

[71] A recent paper by Elsby et al. (2013) finds the countercyclical nature of the NU flows hard to explain; according to those authors, classification errors may only partly explain it and other commonly–cited channels, such as the added worker effect, don't seem to be supported by the data.

(panel C), which would be consistent with our seeing at most a modest inflow of workers into the labor force as the unemployment rate falls.

That said, the most recent data points (the squares) suggest, if anything, a somewhat lower rate of transition into the labor force than is typical at this point in the cycle, although one that is well within the range of past experience. It is possible that, as the recovery continues, transitions into the labor market will be on the correspondingly high side of historic norms, so that on balance the participation rate will move back to a more typical cyclical position. However, another possibility is that the relatively modest flows into the labor force at this point in the cycle are indicative of a greater amount of structural damage, with the result that the labor force rebounds less.

A disaggregated view of the potential cyclical rebound

We can also think about whether some of the withdrawal from the labor market that appears structural might actually be reversed. For instance, as discussed earlier, the share of nonparticipants who report that they want a job is unusually high. If many of them were to return to the labor force, this could result in a greater cyclical rebound than the model currently expects.

A variety of evidence suggests that individuals reporting themselves as out of the labor force but wanting a job do have greater labor force attachment than those who are out of the labor force and do not want a job. As can be seen in panel A of figure 18, the 12-month transition rate into the labor force for a person who is out of the labor force and wants a job is over 40 percent, whereas the transition rate for a non-retired, non-disabled person who is out of the labor force and does not want a job is just above 20 percent.[72]

Correspondingly, individuals who are out of the labor force but want a job also have spent more time working in the recent past than those who are out of the labor force and don't want a job. Using the March Annual Social and Economic Supplement to the CPS we can identify those who report themselves as marginally attached in the basic March survey and then examine their work history during the prior calendar year using the Supplement. This analysis shows that in recent years about 30 percent of those reporting themselves as wanting a job in March worked at least one week in the prior year, compared to less than 10 percent for those who do not want a job. Those reporting themselves as wanting a job were also more likely to have looked for work in the prior year (over 25 percent in recent years, compared to about 2 percent for those not wanting a job). That said, these individuals were still less likely to have looked for work or worked in the prior year than those who reported themselves unemployed at the time of the March survey (about 57 percent of whom engaged in work and or search).

Another way to evaluate the attachment of those not in the labor force but who want a job is to look at their impact on wages. If these individuals are moving in and out of the labor force, even if they search and work less than those who are in the labor force, then they would be expected to put downward pressure on wages. Indeed cross-state evidence suggests as much: A regression of the change in the state median hourly wage on the share of the state population that is out of the labor force and wanting a job (not shown), the share out of the labor force not

---

[72] These 12-month labor force flows as well as those in the discussion of retirement and disability relate to the flows between 5 states: in the labor force, not in the labor force but want a job, retired, disabled, and all other not in the labor force and do not want a job. They are calculated by the authors from the Current Population Survey Longitudinal Population Database (see Nekarda, 2009).

wanting a job and the unemployment rate indicates that those who want a job do put statistically significant downward pressure on wages. A 1 percentage point increase in the share of the population that wants a job holds down wage growth by 0.7 percentage point.[73]

Taken together, this evidence suggests that those who are marginally attached to the labor force in the broad sense do form a potential pool of workers that we might expect to see return. That said, because they constitute a relatively small share of the population, their movement into labor force would likely boost participation by only about ½ percentage point.

Expectations for the future participation rates of younger workers, recent retirees, and the recently disabled

Beyond those who identify themselves as marginally attached, there are other groups of workers whose exit from the labor force may have been prompted by the recession and weak labor market recovery, although in our discussion of the model we attributed their exit to structural factors.

One such group is teenagers and young adults, whose participation rates have dropped dramatically. As noted previously, increased enrollment can explain part of the behavior of recent cohorts. To the extent that lower participation rates for youths are attributable to a rising college premium and greater educational attainment, there are potentially positive effects on the labor force attachment of these cohorts later in life, since participation rates are higher on average for more educated persons. Indeed, the positive effects of additional education could

---

[73] Specifically we regressed the annual percent change in the state median hourly wage from the CPS on the state levels of unemployment, out of the labor force do not want job, and out of the labor force want a job, all divided by the state population, and controls including state and year fixed effects. The observations are weighted by the state 16+ population. This regression is similar to those presented in Christopher Smith "The effect of labor slack on wages: Evidence from state-level relationships," FEDS Notes, Board of Governors of the Federal Reserve System, June 2, 2014.

offset the lost benefits of early work experience. However, we have also witnessed a sharp drop in participation among nonenrollees, which seems more likely to be explained by other factors. In this case, the lack of early labor market experience may have deleterious effects on later labor market experiences for these individuals. As the decline in participation among teens and young adults since 2007 does not primarily appear to be related to a cyclically-induced increase in school enrollment, we probably should not expect the participation rates of these cohorts to rebound substantially beyond the usual effects of aging into their prime working years. That said, it is difficult to pin down the extent to which the low participation of recent cohorts was affected by the deep recession, and so in the projections of the participation rate trend in the next section, we present alternative projections that partly speak to this question

Other groups that might seem to form a potential pool of participants include recent retirees and the disabled. However, the evidence suggests that individuals who retire or become disabled return to the labor market in fairly small numbers, so that even if some of those who transitioned into these state in response to poor job opportunities re-enter as the labor market strengthens further, the effect on the labor force participation rate is likely to be small. As can be seen in panel A of figure 19, over 90 percent of individuals in the survey who report themselves as not in the labor force due to retirement in a given month are in that same state the following year (among those who can be matched); fewer than 4 percent of them are in the labor force a year later (panel B).[74] These flows do suggest transitions from retirement into the labor market are cyclical, apparently rising when expansions are under way and declining as they peak.

---

[74] Maestas (2010) finds that 26 percent of retirees returned to work at some point within six years after their first retirement. Unfortunately, she does not provide information on the length of time that individuals who unretired remained in the workforce. Moreover, the re-entrants are largely concentrated among the youngest retirees, of whom there are few, with a lower (although non-negligible) rate of unretirement among the more numerous older retirees, suggesting that the impact on the aggregate participation rate is not large. Moreover, in most cases (82 percent), this unretirement was planned prior to retirement, rather than being a response to changing economic conditions, such as wealth shocks.

However, even if 12-month flows from retirement into the labor force increased to their pre-recession high of about 4 percent, this would boost the aggregate participation rate by only 0.1 percentage point, all else equal.

Given this evidence, we would only expect greater-than-usual re-entry into the labor force if there was something unique about the current episode. For instance, if many more workers below age 62 had retired than is typical in less severe recessions, we might expect larger flows from retirement into the labor force, since these workers appear to have greater labor force attachment. However, as shown earlier, retirement rates for those under the normal retirement age have not increased since 2007.

The picture is similar for those who report themselves as not in the labor force due to disability: In recent years, nearly 75 percent of individuals who have reported themselves as disabled (figure 19, panel C) and out of the labor force in a given month remained in that state the following year. Moreover, the second most common exit from disability is into retirement (not shown), accounting for 12 percent of transitions, while another 6 percent remain out of the labor force and say they do not want a job, but no longer report themselves as disabled. All told, only 6 to 7 percent of one-year transitions from disability have been into the labor force (panel D), a rate that appears to be trending down, perhaps due to population aging. More striking, data from the Social Security Administration suggest that on average over the 2000's fewer than ½ percent of recipients had their benefits terminated each year due to recipients' earned income, amounting to just a few basis points on the labor force participation rate).[75]

---

[75] While the share of disabled workers exiting due to own earnings is itself cyclical, the range is very small, between 0.42 and 0.56 over 2001 to 2009 period. See O'Leary et al. (2011). Calculations are the authors' own based on estimates in that report and updated information on the number of disabled workers from the SSA.

One final note with respect to retirement in particular, and to a lesser extent disability: the movement of individuals into these states has only a temporary effect on the trend. By age 66, nearly 60 percent of individuals are retired and by age 70 about 70 percent are. Hence, as people age, what might have started as a premature retirement turns into an expected retirement, and the participation rate converges to its trend. This is not to say that there is no cost if people were retiring or entering disability early. There are welfare costs to the individuals involved as well to society as a whole. But the implications for the aggregate labor force participation rate over time are muted.

Model projections

The previous analysis suggests that the cyclical increase in the participation rate as the labor market continues to improve will be at most a little larger than usual, with the most likely entrants to be from the ranks of those who are out of the labor force but want a job and from youths who obtained additional education in response to the weak labor market. Beyond any cyclical effect, the participation rate in coming years will be determined by its trend. We therefore now turn to the model's forecast of the aggregate participation rate.

First, however, we calculate the implications of projected changes in the age distribution alone using equation 1 above, holding the age-specific participation rates constant at their 2014:Q2 values. We use the "middle" projections from the Census Bureau to project the evolution of the age distribution from 2014:Q2 on. Column 1 of table 6 shows the result of this exercise. The changing age distribution alone would be expected to lower the aggregate participation rate a further 2.6 percentage points over the next 10 years.

Table 6: Projections

	Projections		
	1	2	3
	Equation (1)	Model	
		Hold incoming cohort effects and most variables constant	Hold incoming cohort effects constant and extrapolate all other variables
2014:Q2	62.8	63.1	63.1
2015:Q2	62.6	62.9	63.0
2016:Q2	62.3	62.5	62.7
2017:Q2	62.0	62.0	62.4
2018:Q2	61.8	61.5	62.1
2019:Q2	61.6	61.1	61.8
2020:Q2	61.3	60.6	61.5
2021:Q2	61.0	60.2	61.3
2022:Q2	60.7	59.8	61.0
2023:Q2	60.4	59.3	60.7
2024:Q2	60.2	58.9	60.4

Next, we use the baseline model to project the aggregate participation rate, allowing the age-specific trend participation rates to continue to evolve. In terms of the model, the evolution of those age-specific trends depends on the paths of the cohort effects for future cohorts and of the various explanatory variables. Of course, any assumptions for these paths are highly speculative. Nevertheless, they may provide a sense of the range of reasonable projections.

We examine two scenarios. In both, we assume that the unemployment rate falls at its pace of recent years of about ¼ percentage point per quarter until it reaches the CBO's estimate of the long-term natural rate of unemployment in 2015:Q1; we hold the unemployment rate gap at zero thereafter. We project the bankruptcy rate from a linear regression on the unemployment rate gap. In both scenarios, we set the cohort effects for incoming cohorts to the value estimated for the most recent (as of 2014:Q2) cohort of 16-year-olds (i.e., no further declines), extrapolate a continued increase in life expectancies, and allow the Social Security payout rate to evolve according to current law. However, the treatment of the other variables differs between the two scenarios.[76]

The first scenario, shown in column 2, to some extent isolates the implications of the aging of the population by holding the right-hand side variables not mentioned above constant at their last observed levels. This scenario differs from the calculation using equation 1 along several dimensions, but the most important is that, although it holds the incoming cohort effects constant, it allows the existing cohort effects to continue to move through the age distribution as cohorts continue to age. It is this assumption that is mainly responsible for the steeper downward trajectory of the participation rate: Since the young cohorts have lower estimated cohort effects than older ones, they pull down the within-age group participation rates as they age. In the second scenario we (linearly) extrapolate forward each of the variables held constant in the first scenario. The result of this exercise is shown in column 3. In this case, the decline in the aggregate participation rate is similar to that in column1, as factors mentioned earlier – notably increasing longevity and educational attainment and changes in marriage and fertility patterns – continue, offsetting the propagation of the cohort effects.

Beginning from the scenario in column 3, we also imitate the earlier robustness exercises by varying either the number of cohorts included in the estimation or the estimation period. For simplicity, figure 20 shows the baseline projection (omitting the most recent 10 cohorts from the estimation and estimating the model through 2014:Q2) extrapolating the RHS variables as in column 3 of table 6, along with two alternatives: one in which the estimation omits the most recent 15 cohorts and one in which the estimation ends in 2007:Q2. By 2024, the projected participation rates from the two alternatives lie 2½ and 2 percentage points, respectively, above

---

[76] The age effects are, by construction, constant over time in all of the scenarios.

the baseline projection. The differences evident in figures 14 and 16 are amplified as the higher

estimated cohort effects propagate to older ages.[77] Even so, both alternative scenarios eventually

predict further declines in the participation rate from recent values.

Table 7: Comparisons of Projected Labor Force Participation Rates

Year	Authors' Model	Congressional Budget Office	Bureau of Labor Statistics	Social Security Administration	International Monetary Fund
			Labor force participation rate (percent)		
2012	63.7	63.7	63.7	63.7	63.7
2013	63.4	63.3	63.5	63.3	63.3
2014	63.1	62.9	63.3	63.1	63.0
2015	63.0	62.7	63.1	63.2	63.0
2016	62.7	62.5	63.0	63.2	62.9
2017	62.3	62.4	62.7	63.2	62.8
2018	62.1	62.2	62.5	63.3	62.6
2019	61.8	62.0	62.3	63.3	62.3
2020	61.5	61.8	62.0	63.3	-
2021	61.2	61.5	61.8	63.1	-
2022	61.0	61.3	61.6	62.9	-

Sources: Authors' calculations; Congressional Budget Office (2014); Toossi (2013); Social Security
Administration (2014, unpublished data), International Monetary Fund (2014).
Note: Author's projections are for the annual average participation rate, as are those from the CBO, the SSA, and
the International Monetary Fund. BLS projections are for the annual average trend participation rate.

Table 7 compares the projection for the annual average participation rate, based on our

second scenario (column 3 above), to projections developed by several government or

international agencies. In 2014, our projection of the labor force participation rate, at 63.1

percent is similar to that of the other projections. However, over the next eight years, we project

the participation rate to decline 2¼ percentage points to 61 percent, a steeper decline than that

projected by the BLS, CBO or SSA. That said, the differences in the projections are not as stark

---

[77] As noted in section VI, ending the estimation period before the Great Recession robs the bankruptcy variable of
influence. That is why the fitted values from that exercise fall below the baseline until 2012 in figure 20.

as in the 2006 Brookings Paper, in which our 10-year ahead projection for 2015 was 2½

percentage points below that of the next lowest forecast.

VIII. Conclusions

The evidence we present in this paper suggests that much of the steep decline in the labor

force participation rate since 2007 owes to ongoing structural influences that are pushing down

the participation rate rather than a pronounced cyclical weakness related to potential jobseekers'

discouragement about the weak state of the labor market – in many ways a similar message as

was conveyed in the 2006 Brookings Paper. Most prominently, the ongoing aging of the baby-

boom generation into ages with traditionally lower attachment to the labor force can, by itself,

account for nearly half of the decline. In addition, estimates from our model, as well as the

supplementary evidence on which we report, show persistent declines in participation rates for

some specific age/sex categories that appear to have their roots in longer-run changes in the labor

market that pre-date the financial crisis by a decade or more.

In particular, participation rates among youths have been declining since the mid-1990s,

in part reflecting the higher returns to education documented extensively by other researchers,

but also, we believe, some crowding out of job opportunities for young workers associated with

the decline in middle-skill jobs and thus greater competition for the low-skilled jobs traditionally

held by teenagers and young adults. Such "polarization" effects also appear to have weighed on

the participation of less-educated prime-age men and, more recently, prime-age women. In

contrast, increasing longevity and better health status, coupled with changes in social security

rules and increased educational attainment, have contributed to an ongoing rise in the participation rates of older individuals, but these increases have not been large enough to provide much offset to the various downward influences on the aggregate participation rate.

That is not to say that all of the decline in labor force participation reflects structural influences. Our cohort-based model suggests that cyclical weakness was depressing the participation rate by about ¼ percentage point in 2014:Q2, while evidence from cross-state regressions suggests that the contribution of cyclical weakness could be as much as 1 percentage point. The greater cyclicality evidenced in the cross-state regressions could be capturing some of the features of the current labor market we discussed outside the context of the model, such as the unusually high level of those out of the labor force who want a job, or any unusual cyclicality in youth participation or retirement.

Looking ahead, demographics will likely continue to play a prominent role in determining the future path of the aggregate labor force participation rate. The youngest members of the baby-boom generation are still in their early fifties, and thus the effects of population aging will continue to put downward pressure on the participation rate for some time. Indeed, on our estimates, the continued aging of the population alone will subtract 2½ percentage points from the aggregate participation rate over the next ten years. And the overall downtrend could be even larger if some of the negative trends evident for particular age-sex groups persist.

Of course, considerable uncertainty attends these projections. While we can be reasonably sure that the domestic population will age according to Census projections, the future pace of immigration will undoubtedly influence the age distribution of the population, as immigrants are more likely to be in their prime working years than in their 50s or 60s. Moreover, future trends in participation for specific demographic groups are difficult to predict.

Our model has had little success in accurately capturing changes in teenage participation rates, and given the opposing effects of increased school enrollment and polarization, future changes in participation for currently younger cohorts seem especially uncertain. Similarly, while a further uptrend in the participation rates for older individuals seems likely, the pace of that uptrend is difficult to predict.

Moreover, our analysis does not account for general equilibrium feedbacks that may mitigate future declines in participation. For instance, as the downward trend in participation restrains the growth in the labor force, firms may react by increasing real wage rates or otherwise making work more attractive – say, by making work arrangements more flexible – partly offsetting the influence of aging and other factors.

In the end, however, we see further declines in the aggregate labor force participation rate as the most likely outcome. Further improvements in labor market conditions may stem that decline temporarily as discouraged workers are pulled back into the job market, and, indeed, it would not be surprising if the participation rate moved above its trend for a time. Over the longer-term, however, the downward influences on the aggregate labor force participation rate will likely dominate, restraining trend growth in the aggregate labor force and in the growth rate of GDP.

Finally, accepting our conclusion that the aggregate participation will likely decline further over the next decade, it is worth considering the potential implications of this development. The first-order effect, mentioned above, is that—holding trends in population growth (such as migration), average hours worked, and productivity fixed—the nearly 2¼ percentage point decline in the aggregate participation rate we project over the next decade will continue to hold down trend output growth by a little less than ½ percentage point per year through the end of the decade. Another implication is that, as the growth in the labor force slows, the "break-even" level of monthly job gains required to hold the unemployment rate unchanged month-to-month will be lower than decades past. By our calculations, over the next decade somewhere between 50,000 and 75,000 jobs per month will be needed to maintain an unchanged unemployment rate, well less than the amount needed in the 1990s). Of course, these calculations are greatly dependent on the general equilibrium concerns discussed above. More optimistically, for instance, as baby boomers continue to retire, job vacancies may rise in sufficient numbers to mitigate some of the secular downtrend in participation for younger adults and less-educated workers.

References

Aaronson, Daniel, Jonathan Davis, and Luojia Hu. 2012. "Explaining the Decline in the U.S. Labor Force Participation Rate." *Chicago Fed Letter*, Federal Reserve Bank of Chicago, March.

Aaronson, Daniel, Kyung-Hong Park, and Daniel Sullivan. 2006. "The Decline in Teen Labor Force Participation." *Federal Reserve Bank of Chicago Economic Perspectives* 2006Q1: 2-18.

Aaronson, Stephanie, Bruce Fallick, Andrew Figura, Jonathan Pingle, and William L. Wascher. 2006. "The Recent Decline in Labor Force Participation and its Implications for Potential Labor Supply." *Brookings Papers on Economic Activity*, 1:2006.

Acemoglu, Daron and David H. Autor. 2011. "Skills, Tasks, and Technologies: Implications for Employment and Earnings." *Handbook of Labor Economics*, Vol. 4.

Arellano, Manuel and Stephen Bond. 1991. "Some Tests of Specification for Panel Data: Monte Carlo Evidence and an Application to Employment Equations." *Review of Economic Studies*, Vol. 58, No. 2, pp. 227-297.

Autor, David H. 2010. "The Polarization of Job Opportunities in the U.S. Labor Market: Implications for Employment and Earnings." Policy Brief by the *Center for American Progress* and *The Hamilton Project*, April 2010.

Autor, David H. 2011. "The Unsustainable Rise of the Disability Rolls in the United States: Causes, Consequences, and Policy Options." NBER Working Paper No. 17697.

Autor, David H. 2014. "Skills, Education, and the Rise of Earnings Inequality Among the 'Other 99 Percent.'" *Science* 34(6186): 843-851.

Autor, David H. and Mark G. Duggan. 2003. "The Rise in the Disability Rolls and the Decline in Unemployment." Quarterly Journal of Economics, 118(1), February.

Autor, David H. and Mark G. Duggan. 2006. "The Growth in the Social Security Disability Rolls: A Fiscal Crisis Unfolding." *Journal of Economic Perspectives* 20(3): 71-96.

Autor, David H. and David Dorn. 2013. "The Growth of Low-Skill Service Jobs and the Polarization of the US Labor Market." *American Economic Review* 103(5): 1553-1597.

Autor, David H., David Dorn, and Gordon H. Hanson. 2013. "Untangling Trade and Technology: Evidence from Local Labor Markets." *NBER Working Paper* No. 18938.

Balleer, Almut, Ramon Gomez-Salvador, and Jarkko Turunen. 2009. "Labour force participation in the euro area: a cohort based analysis." ECB Working Paper no. 1049, May 2009.

Balleer, Almut, Ramon Gomez-Salvador, and Jarkko Turunen. 2014. "Labour force participation across Europe: a cohort based analysis." Empirical Economics. Vol. 46(4): 1385-1415.

Barnes, Michelle L., Fabià Gumbau-Brisa, and Giovanni P. Olivei. 2013. "Cyclical versus Secular: Decomposing the Recent Decline in U.S. Labor Force Participation." Federal Reserve Bank of Boston, Public Policy Briefs, No. 13-2.

Barnichon, Regis, and Andrew Figura. 2013. "Declining Labor Force Attachment and Downward Trends in Unemployment and Participation." Finance and Economics Discussion Series 2013-88. Board of Governors of the Federal Reserve System (U.S.).

Beaudry, Paul, David A. Green, and Benjamin M. Sand. 2013. "The Great Reversal in the Demand for Skill and Cognitive Tasks." *NBER Working Paper* No. 18901.

Benito, Andrew, and Philip Bunn, "Understanding labour force participation in the United Kingdom." *Bank of England Quarterly Bulletin*, 2011 Q1, pp. 36-42.

Blau, David M. and Ryan M. Goodstein. 2010. "Can Social Security Explain Trends in Labor Force Participation of Older Men in the United States?" Journal of Human Resources, 45(2), March.

Board of Trustees of the Federal Old-Age and Survivors Insurance and Disability Insurance [OASDI] Trust Funds. 2014. "2014 Annual Report of the Board of Trustees of the Federal Old-Age and Survivors Insurance and Disability Insurance Trust Funds." Washington, DC.

Bosworth, Barry P. and Gary Burtless. 2010. "Recessions, Wealth Destruction, and the Timing of Retirement." Center for Retirement Research at Boston College, CRR WP 2010-22.

Charles, Kerwin Kofi, Erik Hurst, and Matthew J. Notowidigdo. 2013. "Manufacturing Decline, Housing Booms, and Non-Employment", NBER Working Paper No. 18949.

Clark, Kim B., and Lawrence H. Summers. 1982. "Labour Force Participation: Timing and Persistence." *Review of Economic Studies*, Vol. 49(2): 825-844.

Congressional Budget Office. 2014. "An Update to the Budget and Economic Outlook: 2014 to 2024." August 2014. Washington, DC.

Council of Economic Advisers. 2014. "The Labor Force Participation Rate Since 2007: Causes and Policy Implications." July.

DiNardo, John, Nicole M. Fortin, and Thomas Lemieux. 1996. "Labor Market Institutions and the Distribution of Wages, 1973-1992: A Semiparametric Approach." *Econometrica*, Vol 64, p. 1001-1044.

Duggan, Mark G. and Scott A. Imberman. 2009. "Why Are the Disability Rolls Skyrocketing? The Contribution of Population Characteristics, Economic Conditions, and Program Generosity." In *Health at Older Ages: The Causes and Consequences of Declining Disability among the Elderly*, NBER conference volume, David M. Cutler and David A. Wise, editors; pp 337-379.

Durand, John D., The Labor Force in the United States 1890-1960. New York: Social Science Research Council, 1948.

Duval-Hernández , Robert, and Pedro Orraca Romano. 2009. "A Cohort Analysis of Labor Participation in Mexico, 1987-2009." IZA Discussion Paper No.4371, August 2009.

Elsby, Michael W.L., Bart Hobijn, and Aysegul Sahin. 2013. "On the Importance of the Participation Margin for Market Fluctuations." Federal Reserve Bank of San Francisco Working Paper Series, 2013-05.

Erceg, Christopher J., and Andrew T. Levin. 2013. "Labor Force Participation and Monetary Policy in the Wake of the Great Recession," IMF Working Paper 13/245, July 2013.

Fallick, Bruce and Jonathan Pingle. 2007. "A Cohort-Based Model of Labor Force Participation." Finance and Economics Discussion Series 2007-9. Board of Governors of the Federal Reserve System (U.S.).

Fujita, Shigeru. 2014. "On the Causes of Declines in the Labor Force Participation Rate." Federal Reserve Bank of Philadelphia, Research Rap.

Gorodnichenko, Yuriy, Jae Song, and Dmitriy Stolyarov. 2013. "Macroeconomic Determinants of Retirement Timing." NBER Working Paper No. 19638.

Hall, Robert. 2014. "Quantifying the Lasting Harm to the U.S. Economy from the Financial Crisis." *NBER Macroeconomic Annual 2014*.

Helman, Ruth, Nevin Adams, Craig Copeland, Jack VanDerhei. 2014. "The 2014 Retirement Confidence Survey: Confidence Rebounds – for Those With Retirement Plans." Employment Benefit Research Institute, Issue Brief No. 397.

Hotchkiss, Julie L., and Fernando Rios-Avila. 2013. "Identifying Factors behind the Decline in the U.S. Labor Force Participation Rate." *Business and Economic Research*, Macrothink Institute, Vol. 3, No. 1, pp. 257-275.

International Monetary Fund, "United States: Selected Issues", IMF Country Report No. 14/222, July 2014,

Jaimovich, Nir and Henry E. Siu. 2012. "The Trend is the Cycle: Job Polarization and Jobless Recoveries." *NBER Working Paper* No. 18334.

Judson, Ruth A. and Ann L. Owen. 1999. "Estimating Dynamic Panel Data Models: A Guide for Macroeconomists." *Economic Letters*, Vol. 65, No. 1, pp. 9-15.

Juhn, Chinhui. 1992. "Decline of Male Labor Market Participation: The Role of Declining Market Opportunities." *Quarterly Journal of Economics* 107(1): 79-121.

Kawata, Hiroshi and Saori Naganuma. 2010. "Labor Force Participation Rate in Japan." *Bank of Japan Review* 2010-E-7, December 2010, pp. 1-9.

Kudlyak, Marianna. 2013. "A Cohort Model of Labor Force Participation." *Economic Quarterly*, Federal Reserve Bank of Richmond, Vol. 99, No. 1, pp. 25-43.

Maestas, Nicole. 2010. "Back to Work: Expectations and Realizations of Work after Retirement." *Journal of Human Resources* 45(3): 718-748.

Mastrobuoni, Giovanni. 2009. "Labor supply effects of the recent social security benefit cuts: Empirical estimates using cohort discontinuities." Journal of Public Economics, 93(11-12), December.

Morisi, Teresa K. 2008. "Youth Enrollment and Employment During the School Year." *Monthly Labor Review* February 2008: 51-63.

Morisi, Teresa K. 2010. "The Early 2000s: A Period of Declining Teen Summer Employment Rates." *Monthly Labor Review* May 2010: 23-35.

Mueller, Andreas I., Jesse Rothstein, and Till M. von Wachter. 2013. "Unemployment Insurance and Disability Insurance in the Great Recession." NBER Working Paper No. 19672.

Nekarda, Christopher J. 2009. "A Longitudinal Analysis of the Current Population Survey: Assessing the Cyclical Bias of Geographic Mobility." Working Paper. http://chrisnekarda.com/2009/05/a-longitudinal-analysis-of-the-current-population-survey/.

O'Leary, Paul, Gina Livermore, and David C. Stapleton. 2011. "Employment of Individuals in the Social Security Disability Programs." *Social Security Bulletin*, Vol. 71, No. 3, pp. 1-10.

Ramey, Gary and Valerie A. Ramey. 2010. "The Rug Rat Race." *Brookings Papers on Economic Activity* Spring 2010: 129-199.

Reifschneider, David, William L. Wascher, and David W. Wilcox. 2013. "Aggregate Supply in the United States: Recent Developments and Implications for the Conduct of Monetary Policy." Finance and Economics Discussion Series 2013-77. Board of Governors of the Federal Reserve System.

Smith, Christopher L. 2011. "Polarization, Immigration, Education: What's Behind the Dramatic Decline in Youth Employment?" *Federal Reserve Board of Governors Finance and Economics Discussion Series* 2011-41.

Smith, Christopher L. 2012. "The Impact of Low-Skilled Immigration on the Youth Labor Market." *Journal of Labor Economics* 30(1): 55-89.

Toossi, Mitra. 2011. "A Behavioral Model for Projecting the Labor Force Participation Rate." *Monthly Labor Review*, May, pp. 25-42.

Toossi, Mitra. 2013. "Labor Force Projections to 2022: The Labor Force Participation Rate Continues to Fall." Monthly Labor Review. Bureau of Labor Statistics. December 2013. Washington, DC.

Van Zandweghe, Willem. 2012. "Interpreting the Recent Decline in Labor Force Participation." *Economic Review*, Federal Reserve Bank of Kansas City, First Quarter 2012, pp. 5-34.